"What a wonderful tool! Like all Wayne Mack's books, *Preparing for Marriage God's Way* is faithfully biblical, thorough, and practical. The priceless bonus with this workbook is its unmatched effectiveness at exposing hidden dangers for engaged couples and providing a platform to help the counselor address them. As a result, couples are much more prepared for the realities of married life."

> —**Marshall L. Asher**, director, Redeemer Counseling Services, San Antonio, Texas

"We've been using *Preparing for Marriage God's Way* for almost ten years now. When I found Wayne Mack's workbook I realized this was exactly what I'd been looking for. I don't perform anyone's wedding without them first going through this workbook with another mentor couple in our church. Over the past ten years, dozens of couples have gone through this material and been given the strong foundation they need for a great and God-glorifying marriage. If you're looking for biblically based premarital material to use in your church or ministry, don't look any further."

> —**Brad Bigney**, pastor; author of *Gospel Treason*

"Wayne Mack's commitment to the sufficiency of Scripture and his years of counseling experience make this book and all his books valuable resources. It is vitally important that people receive biblical instruction going into marriage, and Dr. Mack has provided a most 'helpful' tool."

> —**Bruce Blakey**, pastor, Believers Fellowship, Sa⟨...⟩ ⟨...⟩xas

"God's wonderful gift of marriage is struggling m⟨...⟩ ⟨...⟩d. Christian couples have great opportunities an⟨...⟩ ⟨...⟩orify God as husbands and wives before a watchin⟨...⟩ ⟨...⟩ to take advantage of the opportunity to help these ⟨...⟩ his solemn commitment. Wayne Mack's outstanding ⟨...⟩ ples get to the core issues of marriage. For more than fiftee⟨...⟩ ⟨...⟩ave had couples work through the lessons of this book individu⟨...⟩ and then together. Afterward we spend delightful time reflecting together on their findings. Week by week these men and women become transformed by God's Word to honor the Lord in their new callings as husbands and wives."

> —**John Crotts**, pastor; co-author of *Tying the Knot Tighter* with Martha Peace

"In a culture rife with confusion over the matter of marriage, Dr. Mack brings much needed biblical clarity to the topic. As a pastor, I have found this book an invaluable resource in helping couples prepare to take their marriage journey together. You will find this book a tremendous benefit, whether you are preparing for marriage, or helping to prepare others for marriage, God's way!"

> —**Glenn Dunn**, pastor, Cornerstone Bible Fellowship, North Ridgeville, Ohio

"What if there were a book that could equip engaged couples to identify relational problems before they emerge? What if its solutions were not simply sage advice or psychological theory, but the very Word of God? Every couple would want it. Every pastor would use it. This is that book!"

> —**Daniel Kirk**, senior pastor, Calvary Bible Church, Fort Worth, Texas

"Oh, the problems that could be prevented if couples anticipating marriage worked their way through this book with a caring Christian prior to the wedding ceremony! Wayne Mack's knowledge both of the Scriptures and of marital problem solving is evident in the order of topics; the clear, practical teaching; and the application assignments. If you want to help a couple get off to a good start in marriage, take them through *Preparing for Marriage God's Way*."

> —**Randy Patten**, executive director, National Association of Nouthetic Counselors

"*Preparing for Marriage God's Way* is the most biblical and thorough material I know in helping couples to build their marriage on a firm foundation. I have used the material with numerous young couples, and particularly appreciate the thoughtful discussion questions included in the book that allow both the counselor and the couple to interact on a deep and meaningful level. The book helps the couple anticipate what challenges lie before them in their upcoming marriage, and spurs on conversation that will help them to avoid the 'trouble spots.' . . . I heartily recommend it to both pastors and to those who are preparing for marriage."

> —**Timothy A. Senn**, pastor, The Bible Church of Little Rock

"*Preparing for Marriage God's Way* has been the staple of my pre-marriage counseling for many years. The activities and exercises in this book help couples understand their family of origin and the models that they bring to their marriage. I have found that using this book also helps couples identify the pressure points in their relationship as well as the path forward for resolving the conflicts that occur again and again. This study will get couples into the Word and engaged in conversations they would never have without completing these studies."

—**Tedd Tripp**, president, Shepherding the Heart Ministries

PREPARING
FOR
MARRIAGE
God's Way

PREPARING
FOR
MARRIAGE
God's Way

A Step-by-Step Guide for

Marriage Success

Before and After the Wedding

SECOND EDITION

WAYNE A. MACK

P U B L I S H I N G

P.O. BOX 817 • PHILLIPSBURG • NEW JERSEY 08865-0817

Originally published in 1986 by Hensley Publishing
P&R Publishing edition 2013

Unless otherwise indicated, Scripture quotations are taken from the NEW AMERICAN STANDARD BIBLE ®. © Copyright The Lockman Foundation 1960, 1962, 1963, 1968, 1971, 1972, 1973, 1975, 1977. Used by permission.

Scripture quotations marked (NKJV) are taken from the New King James Version®. Copyright © 1982 by Thomas Nelson, Inc. Used by permission. All rights reserved.

Scripture quotations marked (NIV) are from the HOLY BIBLE, NEW INTERNATIONAL VERSION®. NIV®. Copyright © 1973, 1978, 1984 by International Bible Society. Used by permission of Zondervan Publishing House. All rights reserved.

Italics within Scripture quotations indicate emphasis added.

ISBN: 978-1-59638-929-8 (pbk)
ISBN: 978-1-59638-930-4 (ePub)
ISBN: 978-1-59638-931-1 (Mobi)

Printed in the United States of America

This book is dedicated to the hundreds couples and pastors who have already used the book and have commented on how helpful the material has been to them in their marriages and ministries.

Contents

Foreword

$\mathcal{A}$s indicated by the title, this manual is designed to help you prepare for a God-honoring and personally satisfying relationship in marriage.

Primarily, it was developed to provide you with a carefully outlined, biblical, thorough, and practical tool for helping you to be as ready for marriage as you possibly can.

It has been said that an ounce of prevention is worth a pound of cure and that those who act in haste often sorrow in leisure. It is my sincere prayer and hope that the proper use of this study guide will be a means God uses to diminish the need for the pound of cure and the sorrow and disappointment that often occur when men and women enter into marriage without adequate preparation.

You may use this manual in one of four ways:

1. **Self-directed premarital study course.** In this case, you and your proposed spouse work the through assignments in each of your manuals, then get together to discuss your notes and your answers.

2. **Guided by a marriage counselor.** In this case, the study manual actually provides the basis for the counseling sessions. You and your counselor prepare for each session by studying the material in the manual.

3. **Study guide in group sessions.** A number of couples seriously considering marriage make up a special class for this purpose. In a class setting, the leader uses the manual to teach from and as a format for generating lively discussions. This kind of preparation could be invaluable to you as a couple.

4. **Self-directed study combined with counseling.** In this instance, you first work through each lesson on your own and turn in

9

your exercises to your counselor, who then decides how much individual counseling you need on the basis of your answers.

However you use this manual, it will help you immensely in assessing your marital readiness. It will aid you in uncovering problems that may already exist and will provide you with biblical solutions and guidelines for resolving them.

Preparing for Marriage God's Way will also give you topics for dealing with the inevitable difficulties that will arise after your wedding and encourage you to establish patterns of relating and communicating to resolve conflicts.

Indeed, taking this study seriously could be the launching pad for moving you into a marriage that is truly satisfying and fulfilling. It will certainly prepare you for marriage God's way.

Wayne A. Mack

PART ONE

BEFORE THE WEDDING

Congratulations!

Congratulations are in order because you believe marriage might be in God's plan for your lives together. That is a wonderful thought and one certainly worth investigating.

Congratulations are also in order because you've made the wise decision to spend some time and effort getting ready for marriage. By this time, you may have talked to your pastor about getting married. If you have, he probably has already informed you that he wants to meet with you several times for premarital counseling. Possibly, if there are a number of couples at your stage in their relationship, he has recommended that you join a class designed to prepare people for marriage God's way.

Perhaps your first reaction to this was not all that enthusiastic. But whether you're enthusiastic or less than that, the fact is you're willing to make an effort to prepare for marriage more thoroughly. And that's great!

A lot of couples have never stopped to consider just how important it is to take time to make specific preparation for marriage. When they do, the vast majority of them agree that it makes sense to devote considerable attention to this matter. After all, getting married is one of the most important things you will ever do.

Your pastor, counselor, or teacher will develop the rationale for this endeavor more thoroughly. Indeed, there are good reasons for working through a course of study designed to prepare you for marriage God's way. As you proceed, you will come to believe it to be one of the wisest things you've ever done.

In preparation for your first session, here's what you are to do. Each of you should carefully and prayerfully fill out the following questionnaires. After you've done these exercises individually, share your reflections with each other. Take all the exercises seriously. Make sure you do all the projects thoroughly.

If you're like many who have already completed this course, you'll see an improvement in the quality of your relationship even before marriage. So roll up your sleeves and get ready for a meaningful experience. Carefully do the projects prescribed for session 1. Bring them with you to the session. Be prepared to share the insights you have recorded. And don't hesitate to ask relevant questions.

Assignments:
1. *Relationship History*
2. *Relationship Evaluation*
3. *Marriage Expectation*

RELATIONSHIP HISTORY

1. How long have you known your partner?

2. How did you come to know your partner?

3. List three of your best memories from your dating experience with your partner.

4. List three of your worst memories from your dating experience with your partner.

5. List several kinds of things the two of you like to do together.

6. What place should physical contact and physical involvement play in the relationship of people who are seriously considering marriage? What guidelines or standards should be allowed in this area?

7. What place does physical involvement play in your relationship? Do the two of you agree? Has this been a source of contention or disagreement? If the physical aspect of your relationship were removed, what would be left in your relationship? Is there any guilt or frustration that you have because of your physical involvement during your dating days? How have you maintained a proper balance in reference to expressions of physical affection?

8. What place should the Lord play in a couple's relationship? What place does He play in your relationship? How has and does the Lord make a difference? Do you talk about the Lord together? How do you make Him a vital part of your relationship? How have you worked together to make Him important? Can you honestly say that both of you are closer to being like Jesus because of your relationship with one another? How have you helped each other spiritually? How have you hindered each other spiritually?

9. What do your parents think about your getting married? What is their opinion of your partner? What do your partner's parents think about your getting married? What is their opinion of you? What kind of relationship do you have with them?

10. What should a person tell his or her intended about his or her past? His or her present? His or her sins? Eccentricities? Weaknesses? Struggles? Limitations? How much? What would be legitimate

reasons for sharing? Are there legitimate reasons for not shar-ing? If so, what are they?

In his book *The Secret of Loving,* Josh McDowell writes,

A young man named Chris found himself struggling with this question. After listening to his story, I suggested he not share some of his apparent mistakes with his partner, *unless* his motive for silence was fear—fear that revealing his past would negatively effect the relationship and her love and acceptance of him. If this was his real reason for withholding the information, I would counsel him to share his past with her and to let her love be tested. If the fear was there, he would never feel able to open up to her completely, and it would continue to haunt him.*

Using this criteria, are there any secrets that you should tell your partner?

* Josh McDowell, *The Secret of Loving* (San Bernardino, CA: Here's Life Publishers, 1985), 97.

RELATIONSHIP EVALUATION

1. If you were asked to describe your relationship in one word, what would that word be?

2. What word do you think your partner would use?

3. What are some of the strong points of your relationship?

4. What are some of the weak points of your relationship?

5. What have you done to strengthen these weak points?

6. In your opinion, what do you think are the most important factors that will make a marriage a success? (Be specific and thorough.)

7. What do you bring to the marriage that will help make it a success?

8. What do you think your partner brings to the marriage that will help make it a success?

9. What can a couple do to prepare themselves for marriage? (Be specific and thorough). What have you done specifically to prepare yourself for Christian marriage? What else could or should you do?

MARRIAGE EXPECTATION

1. What thoughts does the word *marriage* bring to you?

2. What are biblical reasons for marriage? Why do you want to get married?

3. What are some goals a couple might have for their marriage? What goals do you have for your marriage? What goals does your partner have for your marriage?

4. What expectations should a person have for his or her spouse in marriage? Why is it important to know specifically what each of you expects from marriage in general, and from each other in particular? What are your expectations for your partner in marriage?

5. What expectations have you had for your partner? How has he or she fulfilled or not fulfilled them?

6. What expectations does your partner have for you in marriage?

7. What expectations has your partner had for you in your relationship? Which ones have you fulfilled or not fulfilled?

2

Going Deeper

"*H*ello! May we have the privilege of introducing you and your partner to you." Perhaps when you read this sentence, you said, "How stupid can you get! I already am well acquainted with myself and my partner."

Well, maybe you are, but since all of us are such complex beings, we can always get to know ourselves and others better. (The truth is the author still has a lot to learn about himself and his wife.) And so you have much to learn about yourself and your partner.

Knowing yourself and your partner in a deep and accurate way is important to the success of your relationship. Understanding yourself and the other person in an intimate and personal way is an essential requirement for developing and maintaining deep unity in your marriage relationship.

This session will help you explore and know yourself and your partner more fully. So roll up your sleeves, begin your effort with fervent prayer, put on your thinking cap, get your Bible, pick up your pen, and go to work.

First, do all the projects by yourself. Write down what you learned about yourself and your partner. Then get together with your partner and discuss your insights. Identify how you felt while you were doing the exercises, while you were discussing them, and now that you have shared the results.

Bring the completed questionnaires with you to your session. Be prepared to give your insights. Be ready to ask questions about anything that you did not fully understand and to raise any concerns that emerged from this assignment.

Assignments:
1. *Reasons for Marriage*
2. *Your Personal Character*
3. *Your Personality*
4. *The Desirable Husband and Wife*
5. *Love's Language*
6. *How Do You Say "I Love You"?*
7. *Common Interests*

REASONS FOR MARRIAGE

1. List ten reasons why you want to marry your partner.

2. How can you know that a certain person is the one for you to marry? What guidelines should be used? What led you to the decision to marry this person? How did you know that you should marry your partner? Why do you think you should marry this person?

3. How important is it for you to find the other person attractive or appealing? What attracts you to or appeals to you about this person?

4. How does 2 Corinthians 6:14–18 relate to the issue of whom to marry? What does it mean to be unequally yoked? Does the person you desire to marry meet the directives given in this passage?

YOUR PERSONAL CHARACTER

On a scale of 0–5, rate yourself and your partner on the following qualities. The highest rating is 5 and 0 is the lowest. For example, if you are very patient, give yourself a 5. If you are not patient at all, give yourself a 0. If you are somewhere in between, rate that between 1 and 4. Circle any area where you and your partner rate more than 1 point difference. Discuss how differences or similarities might affect a marriage relationship.

Qualities	You	Partner
Patient	____	____
Accepting	____	____
Stubborn	____	____
Easily annoyed	____	____
Resentful	____	____
Forgiving	____	____
Dominant	____	____
Self-centered	____	____
Gentle	____	____
Pushy	____	____
A good listener	____	____
Reasonable	____	____
Considerate, thoughtful	____	____
Loner	____	____
Depressive	____	____
Open	____	____
Expressive	____	____
Practical	____	____
Efficient	____	____
Neat, orderly, organized	____	____
Extravagant	____	____

Reliable, dependable   ____   ____

Affectionate   ____   ____

Athletic   ____   ____

Handsome/beautiful   ____   ____

Pleasant voice   ____   ____

Musical   ____   ____

Good dress sense   ____   ____

Forgetful   ____   ____

Lazy   ____   ____

YOUR PERSONALITY

Study the following chart and rate yourself and your partner concerning your personalities. The words numbered 1–3 are to be used to rate yourselves. Use the letter "m" (me) to identify your propensities and the letter "p" to identify your partner's. For example, if you are usually outgoing, rate yourself 2 under the appropriate column on the left side of the page. If your partner is usually reserved, rate him or her a 2 under the appropriate column on the right side of the page. Each of you will have only one rating for each line.

	Slightly — 1	Usually — 2	Always — 3	Slightly — 1	Usually — 2	Always — 3	
Fast							Slow
Outgoing							Reserved
Bold							Timid
Calm							Excitable
Expressive							Unexpressive
Optimistic							Pessimistic
Flexible							Rigid
Artistic							Nonartistic
Athletic							Nonathletic
Loud							Quiet
Logical							Sentimental
Outdoors							Indoors
Trusting							Cautious
Detailed							Generalizer
Specific							Nonspecific
Planner							Disorganized
Loner							People person
Outspoken							Reserved

	Slightly — 1	Usually — 2	Always — 3	Slightly — 1	Usually — 2	Always — 3	
Confident							Insecure
Generous							Frugal
Spender							Saver
Conventional							Unconventional
Practical							Impractical
Initiator							Follower
Responsible							Irresponsible
Punctual							Unpunctual
Aggressive							Passive

Note where you are alike and different. Discuss with your partner ways in which the two of you are quite similar and quite different. Discuss how your similarities and differences have affected your relationship. Discuss what you can do to eliminate any negative effects.

THE DESIRABLE HUSBAND AND WIFE*

Read each statement carefully and then ask yourself, "Is this true of me always (4), often (3), occasionally (2), seldom (1), or never (0)?" Reflect on the meaning of each of the statements. Then write down the number that honestly reflects what is true in your life. Don't overestimate or underestimate (Rom. 12:3). Then go over the sheet again and ask yourself, "Is this true of my partner always (4), often (3), occasionally (2), seldom (1), or never (0)?" Write down the number that honestly reflects your evaluation of your partner's life. Compare how the two of you are alike and different—your relative strengths and weaknesses. Think about and discuss the implications of your ratings for your marriage.

	You	Partner
1. I am fully devoted to God; I have a deep and meaningful relationship with God.	____	____
2. I am loving.	____	____
3. I am joyful.	____	____
4. I am peaceful.	____	____
5. I am longsuffering.	____	____
6. I am gentle.	____	____
7. I am generous, willing to share.	____	____
8. I am kind.	____	____
9. I am faithful, trustworthy, dependable.	____	____
10. I am self-controlled, disciplined.	____	____
11. I am noble in character.	____	____
12. I am respected and valued by my family.	____	____
13. I am devoted and loyal to my family.	____	____
14. My family can depend on me.	____	____
15. I fulfill God-given family responsibilities.	____	____
16. I receive praise from my family and others.	____	____
17. I build up my family; I am an encourager.	____	____

* Based on Galatians 5:22,23; 1 Peter 3:1–7; Proverbs 31:10–31

18. I am devoted to ministering to others. ____ ____

19. I am consistent and steadfast in doing right. ____ ____

20. I am an industrious, hard worker. ____ ____

21. I am unselfish. ____ ____

22. I am more concerned about internal beauty than external beauty. ____ ____

23. I take care of myself physically; I am concerned about my appearance, but not excessively so. ____ ____

24. I am able to enjoy life; I am not a workaholic; I am not overly intense or serious; I am a fun person to be with. ____ ____

25. I am contented and satisfied; I desire growth, progress, and biblical change but am not overbearing about it. ____ ____

26. I am courageous and confident. ____ ____

27. I am considerate of others, putting them at ease, and communicating respect and concern for them. ____ ____

28. My speech is constructive and wholesome. ____ ____

29. I seek to grow in wisdom, to sharpen myself intellectually. ____ ____

30. I exercise foresight; I plan ahead. ____ ____

31. I handle money wisely; I practice good stewardship. ____ ____

LOVE'S LANGUAGE*

Rate yourself and your partner on the following ways in which each of you desires to have love shown to you. Use a scale of 1–8, with 1 being the most important and 7 or 8 being the least important.

If, in your case, the most important way in which you want to have love shown to you is by having the other person touch you, caress you, cuddle you, and kiss you, that would be number 1. You would then put the number 1 in the *You* column beside the number 4 statement. If in your partner's case, you think (do this without asking) helping is the most important factor, then that would be number 1. You would write the number 1 in the *Partner* column beside statement 1.

Continue rating the other items in order of importance. If, in your view, something that is not listed is very important, identify it on line 8 and give it the rating you think it deserves.

In answer to the completion questions that follow the rating exercise, write out your honest opinions. Think about why this project is important and how understanding these things could help your marriage. Consider also how a lack of understanding of these issues could affect a marriage.

	You	Partner
1. Helping	____	____
2. Spending time together, being there, doing things together, being willing to communicate	____	____
3. Saying it with words, expressing appreciation and admiration	____	____
4. Touching, caressing, kissing, physical contact	____	____
5. Being concerned about opinions, feelings, interests, desires, likes, dislikes; being cooperative, solicitous; listening; sharing	____	____

* Adapted from Judson J. Swihart, *How Do You Say "I Love You"? 8 Languages of Love* (Downers Grove, IL: InterVarsity Press), 1977.

6. Being loyal, faithful, protective, trustworthy, supportive, unselfish, responsible; keeping confidences; fulfilling promises and commitments   ____   ____

7. Meeting material and physical needs, taking care of possessions, giving gifts, giving birthday or anniversary cards, trading places, doing fix-it jobs, etc.   ____   ____

8. Other: ____   ____

HOW DO YOU SAY "I LOVE YOU"?

Complete each of the following sentences in one or more ways:

1. During childhood, I knew my parents loved me because they:

2. When down, I like my partner to:

3. After an argument, I want my partner to:

4. I gain a strong sense of inner comfort when my partner:

5. I have strong affectionate feelings when my partner:

6. I wish my partner would more frequently:

7. If I wanted to feel loved, I would ask my partner to:

8. The nicest gift I ever received from my partner was when:

9. When I want to really show my love to my partner, I:

10. The most meaningful thing a person could ever do for his or her partner is:

11. I feel acceptance and worth when my partner:

12. What I like best about myself is:

13. What I like best about my partner is:

14. What I like least about myself is:

15. What I like least about my partner is:

16. Two of the happiest things that have ever happened to me are:

17. Two of the happiest things that have ever happened to my partner are:

18. The hardest experience I have ever had is:

19. The hardest experience my partner has ever had is:

20. If I could do anything I wanted and knew that God would provide all the resources and guarantee success, I would:

21. If my partner could do anything he or she wanted and knew that God would provide the resources and guarantee success, he or she would:

22. My greatest fear is:

23. My partner's greatest fear is:

24. Five things that I really enjoy doing are:

25. Five things that my partner enjoys doing are:

COMMON INTERESTS

How do you and your partner take part in the following activities? Check the appropriate space for each item. It is possible that neither of you does some of the activities. In those cases, you may get some ideas of activities to try together.

	Together	Both But Not Together	One Exclusively	One Primarily	Neither
Church (attendance and service)					
Reading					
Competitive sports (tennis, volleyball, etc.)					
Spectator sports					
Noncompetitive sports (jogging, swimming, etc.)					
Outdoor activities (camping, walking, etc.)					
Social gatherings (family, friends, church, community, etc.)					
Clubs, organizations					
Art appreciation (listening to music, visiting museums, etc.)					
Creative and interpretive art (writing, painting)					
Hobbies (collecting, gardening, sewing, woodwork, etc.)					
Business and professional activity					

	Together	Both But Not Together	One Exclusively	One Primarily	Neither
School functions or organizations					
Politics					
Movies					
Devotions					
Shopping					
Table games					
Sightseeing *(traveling)*					
Entertaining friends					
Other:					

3

Real Love

*Y*ou're in love. Right? Well, that's great! Being in love is a wonderful experience. It's also a very crucial factor in a successful marriage. In fact, it's so important that if you don't really love each other your marriage will be a disaster.

When people fail to love or be loved, all sorts of horrible things may occur. Without love, life often becomes unbearable, personal problems become overwhelming, relationships deteriorate, marriages fall apart, and families disintegrate.

Jesus certainly underscored the fundamental importance of love in His summary of what God desires of us. He said, " 'You shall *love* the LORD your God with all your heart, and with all your soul, and with all your mind.' This is the great and foremost commandment. The second is like it, 'You shall *love* your neighbor as yourself.' On these two commandments depend the whole Law and the Prophets" (Matt. 22:37–40).

Now, most people would wholeheartedly agree that to have a good marriage two people must love each other. However, at that point their agreement about love would often end.

Ask ten different people for a definition of *love* and you might get ten different answers. Or, what is perhaps even more tragic, you might get no answers. Very often those who talk most about love don't seem to have much of an idea of what love is.

People get married because they say they love each other. Unfortunately, many of them cannot define love, or they have an erroneous or inadequate understanding of what love is.

51

How can you know if you are in love without a correct understanding of what you claim to be experiencing? How can you know if you are loving or being loved if you don't know what real love is? The truth is, you can't.

And that's a serious problem in many relationships. That's why many people who think and say they're in love don't act very loving. That's why many marriages that begin with high expectations end in disaster. People thought they were in love, but they didn't know the essence of love.

So the question of what it means to really love someone is a significant question. It's one that you and every couple who aspires to marriage should seriously consider. It's a question to which you should have some definite, solid answers.

Some tell us that real love can't be explained. It can only be experienced. Now, this statement is both true and false. It's true in that real love, God's kind of love, goes beyond explanation. It's false in that God, who knows all things, has given us some very clear statements in the Bible about the nature and essence of love.

Perhaps by this time, you're saying, "Come on, you've told us that love is important. We agree. You've stated that God does give definite information about what love is. What you haven't done is give us that information."

Well, thank you for raising that issue. That's precisely what this session is designed to accomplish. At this time, I want you to devote your attention to the crucial issue of what our infallible, all knowing, gracious God says about real love. Get ready to be challenged.

Assignment:

1. *Understanding True Love.* As you complete the worksheet, seek to answer two questions:

   a. What is love?

   b. How can I demonstrate my love to others?

Additional study:

For a more in-depth study of what biblical love is and isn't, see Wayne Mack's book *Maximum Impact: Living and Loving for God's Glory* (Phillipsburg, P&R Publishing, 2010).

UNDERSTANDING TRUE LOVE

Searching Scripture

Look up the following passages of Scripture and write down what each of them indicates about true love. Note carefully what love isn't as well as what it is, what it doesn't do as well as what it does do. Note also the implicit as well as the explicit statements.

1. Proverbs 10:12

2. Matthew 5:43–48

3. Romans 13:8–10

4. Romans 14:14–15

5. Galatians 5:13–15

6. Ephesians 5:25

7. 1 Thessalonians 4:9–10

8. 1 Timothy 1:5

9. Titus 2:3–4

10. I John 3:16–18 (see also James 2:15–16)

Going In-depth

I Corinthians 13 is the great love chapter of the Bible. No discussion of love would be complete without a study of this chapter. I Corinthians 13 describes God's kind of love, a kind of love that a Christian may have and express because of what God is doing and has done for and in him or her. Study particularly verses 4–7, and write down the different elements of love. Beside each element explain what that element means in your own words. After trying to identify the meaning on your own, check a good commentary to get additional insights. Then, having written down the meaning of the phrase, recount at least one example from your relationship with your partner of how you can show this facet of love to your prospective spouse.

Here are two examples:

I CORINTHIANS 13 STATEMENT: "love suffers long" (v. 4 NKJV)
    Meaning: Love is not impatient or nasty. Love is not fretful or intolerant. Love is patient, willing to suffer long without retaliating. Love gives

the other person space. Love is willing to wait. Love doesn't manipulate or sinfully pressure the other person into changing.

Examples: When my partner doesn't see things the way I see them, loving him or her means I will not try to coerce agreement with me by the loudness of my voice, or by threats, or by being critical or silent, or by withdrawing. Love means that I will allow my partner to think differently. I will not attempt to overpower or force conforming to me.

1 CORINTHIANS 13 STATEMENT: "[love] keeps no record of wrongs" (v. 5 NIV)

Meaning: Love forgives even when forgiveness is not requested, Love does not stew about the past. It chooses not to remember what lies behind. Love views each day as a new day and does not allow the past to ruin it. Love doesn't continue to review the ways my partner has offended me. Love keeps a record of the good things my partner does.

Examples: I will not hold a grudge or refuse to forgive my partner even when he or she repeatedly is late for our dates. I will not continue to think about the times when my partner forgets to do something I ask. Instead, I will think of the way my partner smiles when he or she sees me, or the way he or she prays for me, or how he or she is helpful.

Your own work: (You may even want to redo the samples by giving other examples that are more appropriate to your life and relationship. Write in the verse and then the statement as in the examples.)

1 CORINTHIANS 13 STATEMENT:

Meaning:

Examples:

1 CORINTHIANS 13 STATEMENT:

Meaning:

Examples:

1 CORINTHIANS 13 STATEMENT:

Meaning:

Examples:

1 CORINTHIANS 13 STATEMENT:

Meaning:

Examples:

1 CORINTHIANS 13 STATEMENT:

Meaning:

Examples:

1 CORINTHIANS 13 STATEMENT:

Meaning:

Examples:

1 CORINTHIANS 13 STATEMENT:

Meaning:

Examples:

1 CORINTHIANS 13 STATEMENT:

Meaning:

Examples:

1 CORINTHIANS 13 STATEMENT:

Meaning:

Examples:

1 CORINTHIANS 13 STATEMENT:

Meaning:

Examples:

1 CORINTHIANS 13 STATEMENT:

Meaning:

Examples:

1 CORINTHIANS 13 STATEMENT:

Meaning:

Examples:

1 CORINTHIANS 13 STATEMENT:

Meaning:

Examples:

Evaluating You

Evaluate yourself as your partner's lover by using the criteria about real love that you have just defined and illustrated. Read each statement carefully and then ask yourself, "Is this true of me always (4), often (3), occasionally (2), seldom (1), or never (0)?"

1. I am longsuffering. ____
2. I am kind. ____
3. I am contented; I am happy when my partner has something that I don't. ____
4. I don't try to impress my partner with how great I am and how lucky he or she is to have me. ____
5. I understand that whatever gifts I have are by God's grace; I am not proud; I am not haughty or arrogant, thinking that I am superior to my partner; I consider his or her views and needs to be as important as mine. ____

6. I am not rude; I don't act unbecomingly; I am courteous and polite; I am considerate; I am mannerly and tactful.   _____

7. I do not seek my own; I am not self-centered; I am not opportunistic or manipulative; I am willing to sacrifice; I am willing to change; I am genuinely concerned about my partner; I serve my partner.   _____

8. I don't enjoy making fun of my partner or exposing his or her faults; I affirm and express appreciation to my partner; I am not critical; I bring out the best in my partner.   _____

9. I am willing to forgive; I don't hold grudges; I don't keep a record of wrongs; I am willing to live in the present with my partner; I don't remind him or her of past mistakes.   _____

10. I am loyal, faithful, and trustworthy; I seek to protect my partner; I am willing to share and carry his or her burdens and problems; I keep confidences.   _____

11. I recognize my own faults and the faults of my partner but still maintain a positive, hopeful attitude; I am not moody.   _____

12. I am slow to anger; I am not easily annoyed or irritated with my partner; I control the expression of my anger; I don't attack my partner but seek to deal with the problem.   _____

13. I am not suspicious; I trust my partner; I have confidence in him or her; I treat him or her with respect; I'm not constantly demanding assurance and reaffirmation.   _____

14. I am committed to my partner; I will persevere in this relationship; I will be steadfast; I hang in there; I am consistent in acting toward my partner in a loving way; I realize that love is a choice I make and is not exclusively a matter of feelings or emotions; I choose to love even when I don't feel very loving.   _____

Improving as a Lover

Now that you have evaluated your love quotient, list all of the items that you scored 0–2. No one except Jesus Christ or the people who are already in heaven could score all 4s. Every one of us falls short of this standard, but it is the standard. God will not allow us to lower the standard just because we don't reach it.

After you have identified the facets of love in which you are most deficient, acknowledge your deficiencies to Christ and ask Him for forgiveness. But more than that, ask Him for His help in improving as real lovers. Christ is your Example and your Enabler. By His power, you can improve if you really want to. You can change if you are willing to recognize your failure, seek His power, and specifically make plans about how you can improve.

Think about what you could do in practical ways to make sure you maintain and even develop more fully the facets of real love described in 1 Corinthians 13. Study the Bible to discover how love is developed and maintained. Write a brief article summarizing your discoveries. Be prepared to share your insights in the session. Be ready also to ask your counselor or teacher for suggestions about improving as a lover.

1. List of love deficiencies:

2. Plan for improving as a lover:

Serving One Another

Make a list of the legitimate longings and desires of your partner. Think of his or her total life—physical, intellectual, spiritual, social, emotional, financial, recreational, etc. What does he or she need and/or want in these areas? We have seen that love involves helping other people, but you probably won't help unless you know where they need help. Don't sit around and wait for your partner to tell you. *You* have to be aggressive. Look for and plan ways to serve one another.

Physical Needs and/or Wants:

What I can do to fulfill these needs or desires:

Intellectual Needs and/or Wants:

What I can do to fulfill these needs or desires:

Spiritual Needs and/or Wants:

What I can do to fulfill these needs or desires:

Emotional Needs and/or Wants:

What I can do to fulfill these needs or desires:

Social Needs and/or Wants:

What I can do to fulfill these needs or desires:

Financial Needs and/or Wants:

What I can do to fulfill these needs or desires:

Recreational Needs and/or Wants:

What I can do to fulfill these needs or desires:

Other Needs and/or Wants:

What I can do to fulfill these needs or desires:

Serving Your Partner

Write down what you are presently doing to serve your partner. Add to that list specific, tangible things that you might do.

1. Record how you are presently serving your partner.

2. List other ways you may serve your partner and show love to him or her.

4

God's Blueprint for Marriage

arriage is a divine institution. It is God's idea. He made the first man and woman. He introduced them to each other. He gave them their premarital counseling. He performed the first wedding service. Without a doubt, He knows best what marriage should be and how married people should conduct their relationship.

Getting to know what marriage is, God's way, should be of great concern for every couple considering marriage. As two people sincerely and earnestly attempt to follow the blueprint He has outlined in His Word, they will find success and true happiness. The purpose for this session is to help the two of you learn together about God's plan for marriage.

An important concept to consider in preparing for marriage is the necessity of leaving your father and mother. You have already been directed to think seriously about this crucial part of God's plan for marriage. But you should go still further in exploring this issue by using the practical exercises found on the next few pages.

Assignments:
First do each of these studies individually. Then get together and discuss your individual ideas.

1. *Families of Origin Study*
2. *In-Law Relations*

3. *In-Law Inventories 1 and 2*

4. *Commitment in Marriage Study*

Additional study:

For further help dealing with in-law relations, see Wayne Mack's booklet *In-Laws: Married with Parents* (Phillipsburg, P&R Publishing, 2009).

FAMILIES OF ORIGIN STUDY

Discuss together the similarities and differences between your families. Write down your findings. Make sure you discuss the following items.

1. Family occupations (blue-collar vs. white-collar, both parents work or just one, etc.)

2. Marriage of parents (good, fair, bad, poor, still together, divorced, separated, etc.)

3. Family rules (for example, "children should not argue with parents," "children do the dishes," etc.)

4. Personality features and characteristics of mother and father

5. Family beliefs (for example, "the family that prays together stays together," "cleanliness is next to godliness," etc.)

6. Views about finances (how money should be spent, saved, etc.)

7. Views about sex (often discussed, never discussed, dirty subject, etc.)

8. Views about responsibilities and roles of the husband/father and wife/mother (for example, "Mom always does the dishes," "Mom always cleans the house," "Dad mows the lawn," "Dad makes the decisions," etc.)

9. Relationships with extended families (grandparents, uncles, etc.)

10. Involvement in church activities, spiritual things, etc.

11. Family political views

12. Views about work, recreation, and vacations

13. Family secrets (for example, Aunt Mary was pregnant when she married, Uncle John had a drinking problem, etc.)

14. Ways of handling problems, disagreements; ways of communicating

15. Family values or standards

16. Family boundaries (personal privacy issues; ideas about personal possessions, freedom to be an individual, liberty to have own

interests, make own decisions; extent to which other people were allowed into family affairs; expressions of affection; attitudes toward fun, etc.)

Answer the following questions.

1. How are your families of origin alike and different?

2. How are your mothers and fathers alike and different?

3. What impact has your family background had on you positively and negatively? In what specific ways have you been affected?

4. How may your future marriage and marriage partner be affected either directly or indirectly?

IN-LAW RELATIONS

1. Do you have any problems with your parents or your prospective in-laws? Write down the kinds of problems you have had.

2. What kinds of in-law problems have you observed in the marriages of others?

3. What are the most common mistakes that in-laws (children and parents, brothers-in-law, sisters-in-law, etc.) make?

4. Study Exodus 18, the description of Moses' relationship with his father-in-law, and write down everything you see about the kind of relationship that Jethro and Moses had. Try to discern why this was such a good relationship.

5. Turn to the book of Ruth and do the same in reference to the relationship of Ruth and Naomi. What characteristics of Naomi should a mother-in-law model, and what characteristics of Ruth should a daughter-in-law model?

6. Taking what you have just learned from the Bible, imagine that someone has come to you asking for your advice about how to develop a good relationship with his or her present or prospective in-laws. Write out what you would say.

7. Identify what you could do to improve your relationship with
    your prospective in-laws.

8. Write a letter to your prospective in-laws expressing appreciation for them and indicating the kind of relationship you want to have with them.

9. Write a letter to your parents expressing your views on how you should relate to them, and they to you and your spouse after marriage. A sample is included on the next page. Read this carefully and then develop a letter of your own. Bring your letter with you to the next session.

SAMPLE LETTER: CHILD TO PARENTS

Dear Mom and Dad,

I want to thank you for your love and devotion to me as I was grow-ing up. You have been good parents, bringing me up in the counsel and the discipline of the Lord. You have been used by God to make me what I am. Through you, your words, your actions, reactions, and attitudes, I have learned. To you I am deeply indebted and grateful and will always be.

At this time, a very important time in each of our lives, our rela-tionship will change—not deteriorate but change, not disappear but be altered. Scripture asserts that for the cause of marriage shall a man leave his mother and father. Well, that time has arrived in my life. As a Christian I will always honor you, appreciate you, respect you, pray for you, commend you, and seek to help you, but still God says I must leave. And in obedience to the God I love I will do that.

God says that next to my relationship to Him—or perhaps I should say as part of my relationship to Him—my relationship with my wife/husband must become the priority relationship in life. I am sure you will agree.

From the time of our wedding onward _____ and I will become one flesh.

We want to have the relationship God intends and to be everything God wants us to be. I ask you to regard _____ as a part of the family in the same way as you regard me. After all, the Bible says we have become one flesh and he who loves his wife loves himself. I ask you to help us to learn how to merge our two independent lives into a one-flesh relationship practically.

You have been given wisdom from God and from time to time we will be turning to you for counsel. When we do, we will take your counsel seriously, but under God we will think, search the Scriptures, pray, and determine God's will for ourselves. We want, we need your continued love and assistance, but God has called us to establish a new family for Christ, developing our own unique lifestyle within the framework of the Scriptures. We want to be your friends as well as your children. We want you to be free to agree or disagree with us and love us regardless. We want the same freedom. This will be hard for us and for you. After all, until this point under God you have been my number one authority in life. I have come to depend upon you, to look first to you for counsel and support and assistance. Now that changes, and change is hard, for me and for you.

Please understand what I am saying—I/we want to be what God wants. I/We want our relationship with you to be a good one. I/We love you deeply, respect you greatly, and are expecting that the future will bring new and enjoyable aspects to our relationship. Thanks again for all you are and have been to us. We love you.

Son/Daughter

IN-LAW INVENTORY 1

RATING SCALE:
2 = Very much
1 = Some
0 = Not at all

	You	Partner
Excessive dependence upon parents	____	____
Jealous of partner's relationship with parents	____	____
Critical of partner's parents and/or relatives	____	____
Gossips to parents about partner	____	____
Critical of partner to parents	____	____
Takes sides with parents against partner	____	____
Excessive talking about parents	____	____
Compares partner to parents	____	____
Is partial to own parents	____	____
Puts parents above partner	____	____
Favorably compares own parents to partner's parents	____	____
Makes plans with parents without seeking partner's counsel or advice	____	____
Allows parents to dominate	____	____
Excessive desire to please parents	____	____

Now summarize what impressed you about yourself and your partner in relationship to your parents.

IN-LAW INVENTORY 2

RATING SCALE:
2 = Very much
1 = Some
0 = Not at all

	Your Parents	Partner's Parents
Find fault	_____	_____
Meddle in our affairs	_____	_____
Have unrealistic expectations of our relationship	_____	_____
Are overly possessive and protective in our relationship	_____	_____
Are indifferent and aloof toward us	_____	_____
Are overly dependent upon child	_____	_____
Gossip about us	_____	_____
Insist on having their own way	_____	_____
Talk too much	_____	_____
Won't listen	_____	_____
Are unappreciative	_____	_____
Are jealous of other set of parents	_____	_____
Are jealous of our relationship with other people	_____	_____

Now summarize what impressed you about your parents and prospective in-laws through this study.

COMMITMENT IN MARRIAGE STUDY

1. Read Numbers 30:2, Deuteronomy 23:21, Psalm 15:4b, and Ecclesiastes 5:4. What do these passages teach about making commitments?

2. Consider the following statement of commitment.

Sample statement: As I marry you, I am making a lifelong and irrevocable commitment to know and love God and to know and love you. I can learn to love you only as I come to know God's love for me. I therefore commit myself to daily seek to know God better by asking Him to teach me as I meditate on His Word.

I promise never to stop seeking to learn how to love you better. I want my love to duplicate the love described in 1 Corinthians 13. I want my love for you to be patient, kind, and enduring, not jealous or envious; a love that is content with what God is pleased to give us; a love that is not proud or selfish, not rude or inconsiderate; a love that is gentle with your weaknesses and seeks to point you to Christ, not me; a love that responds graciously when we have a disagreement. Most of all, I want my love to be a love that points you to the source of all real love, our Savior Jesus Christ.

I commit myself to seek with God's certain help to love you with a love that overlooks annoying wrongs, failures, sins, or inconsistencies, being glad to forgive and remembering that I have probably wronged and failed you more times than you have wronged or failed me; a love that remembers that I have wronged Jesus greatly and yet He died for me and forgave me; a love that is grieved when you are hurt or troubled or sinful and that reaches out to give appropriate help, to restore and uplift rather than demean, despise, expose, or condemn.

By God's grace, I resolve to love you with a love that does not demand its own way; a love that is creatively thoughtful and looks for ways to encourage; a love that is not self seeking, putting your needs before my own. I promise to protect you and stick with you. I will believe the best about you and seek to put the best interpretation on your actions and motives.

I pledge myself to a love that will know no limit to its trust, no fading of its hope; a love that will stand when all else around us has fallen. I covenant to give myself wholly to you and to pursue an exclusive intimacy with you. I dedicate myself to finding my ultimate contentment and satisfaction in Jesus Christ and not to seeking it from you or from any other source.

I promise to share with you daily my thoughts, my dreams, my hopes, my joys, my successes, my troubles, my fears, my failures, all of my life. More than that, I will encourage you to share yourself with me—your thoughts, dreams, hopes, joys, successes, troubles, fears, and failures, all of your life. And when you do, I will listen and care and share.

I pledge to give God the glory for anything good that He does through me. I marry you with the conviction that to be a good husband/wife, I must know, worship, and serve God first of all. I, therefore, make all these commitments with the understanding that I must first of all be committed wholeheartedly to God; by His grace, that I am, and, by His grace, that I will continue to be. This is my commitment to God and to you.

Are you ready to make a commitment such as this?

Yes   _____

I'm not sure   _____

No   _____

Signed _____

a. Write out the basic factors or principles that are included in it.

b. What would you include from this statement in your own marriage commitment?

c. What would you add to this statement?

d. What would you delete from it? How would you change it?

3. And now, having examined this sample commitment statement, build on the work you have just done. Write a statement describing your commitment to your partner by completing this statement: "I realize that the essence of marriage is commitment to God and to you. As I marry you, I commit myself . . ."

Make your statement personal and specific. Of course, you may use elements from the sample statement. But don't just copy it verbatim. Put your commitment in your own words. Make it a reflection of your understanding of what the Bible says about your responsibilities and privileges in marriage. Include your convictions about how you will fulfill and apply these principles in your relationship.

5

Your Most Important Relationship

For the past few weeks, you and your counselor or teacher have been discussing how to prepare for marriage God's way. You talked about your reasons for wanting to get married. You reflected on your similarities and differences. You considered God's plan for marriage and discussed the practical implications of that plan for your relationship.

In the weeks that lie ahead, you will be expanding your studies into still other important areas. In particular, you will be looking at the important subjects of communication in marriage, conflict resolution, husband and wife roles, finances, and sex.

By this time you've become aware of the fact that a good marriage won't just drop out of the sky on your wedding day. Successful marriages require work—and lots of it.

Good marriages are based on commitment. They are the fruit of a commitment to God and His plan for marriage. They are the by-product of a commitment to:

1. the priority of the marriage relationship,

2. the development of a partnership and friendship in the marriage relationship,

3. the permanence of the marriage relationship,

4. the expenditure of whatever effort is necessary and biblically legitimate to make the marriage successful,

5. the duty to serve and help each other grow and develop into the person God wants each of you to be.

Face the fact that good marriages are not easy to develop or maintain. In good marriages people have problems, but they don't run away from them. Rather, they stay and work through those problems in a loving and gentle way.

Believe it or not, there may be times when you will not feel like loving your spouse. Occasionally you may not feel like serving. Now and then you may not feel like working through problems. Sometimes the thing you may feel like doing most is tucking your tail under your back legs and running away as fast as you can.

When that occurs, where will you find the motivation and the strength to make your marriage a success? What will encourage and empower you to hang in there and do what you ought to do regardless of how you feel?

There's only one real answer to that question: a deep and vital relationship with Jesus Christ. This is the only thing that will give you strength and motivation to hang in there and solve your problems.

Jesus must be your support in times of trouble. He must be your trusted advisor and constant companion. He must be your ultimate reason for living. He must be your sufficiency, your all in all. He must be the One who enables you to keep your marriage commitment when the going gets tough.

What this means is that to have a marriage God's way, you must make your relationship with Jesus Christ a priority matter. Never let anything or anyone come between you and your Lord! Never allow anything or anyone to pull you away from His arms of love.

Stay close to Him, come what may. Personally spend time each day in His Word and in prayer. Devote yourselves as a couple to regular practice of Bible study and worship. Dedicate yourselves to meeting faithfully with other believers to encourage and be encouraged, to minister and to receive ministry. Make involvement in a biblical church a priority issue in your lives. "Draw near to God and he will draw near to you" (James 4:7 NKJV).

Mark it down as a basic axiom for your marital success: *your relationship with God is the most important relationship in your relationship with each other.* Make sure you don't neglect it.

This session has been planned to facilitate three primary goals. First, this session will aid you in personally evaluating and enlarging this most basic and important of all your relationships. Second, it will help you explore your similarities and differences in terms of your relationship with God and your spiritual convictions. Third, it has been designed to assist you in developing a spiritual growth and development strategy for you as a married couple.

So roll up your sleeves, begin your effort with fervent prayer, put on your thinking cap, pick up your Bible and a pen, find a quiet place, and go to work.

Assignments:
1. *Your Spiritual Convictions.* This questionnaire will help you evaluate your own spiritual life. It will also help you see where the two of you are alike and different in your spiritual lives.
2. *Your Prayer Life*
3. *You and Your Bible*

YOUR SPIRITUAL CONVICTIONS

Finish the following sentences with two or three answers each.

    1. God is:

    2. Jesus Christ is: *(describe who you think He is, what He has done, what He is doing now, what place He has in your life, what He means to you, etc.)*

3. My relationship to God and His Son Jesus Christ is: *(describe the kind of relationship you have with God and how important that relationship is—be specific)*

4. A Christian is:

5. I know that I am (or am not) a Christian because:

6. The Bible is: *(describe what you think it is, what it means to you, what place it has in your life, how you use it, etc.)*

7. Sin is:

8. My chief sins are:

9. When I sin, I: *(describe how you handle sin, what you feel when you sin, what you do after you sin)*

10. I feel guilty when:

11. I pray: *(when, how, why, what for, etc.)*

12. My chief goals in life are:

13. I want (or do not want) to attend and be involved in church: *(answer the questions "how" and "why")*

14. I believe fellowship with other Christians is: *(define what it is, what it involves, how important it is, and how it can be developed)*

15. I am promoting my spiritual growth and the spiritual growth of my partner by:

16. My partner and I differ in spiritual matters: *(when, how, over what, etc.)*

17. The changes I would like to make in my own spiritual life are:

18. The changes I would like my partner to make spiritually are:

Review your answers. Are there any that you would like to change? Which ones? Why? Are there any to which you do not know the answer? Which ones? Compare and discuss your answers with your partner. Write down your impressions of this study. What have you learned about yourself and what have you learned about your partner? What changes do you need to make in light of this study?

YOUR PRAYER LIFE

1. How would you characterize your prayer life?

    a. Very satisfactory

    b. Satisfactory

    c. Satisfactory but needing improvement

    d. Unsatisfactory

    e. Very unsatisfactory

2. Briefly state your reasons for answering question 1 as you did.

3. On a scale from 0–10, with 10 being the highest rating, how important do you consider prayer in the Christian life?   ____

4. On a scale of 0–10, how important is prayer in your actual practice?   ____

5. If you think your prayer life should be improved, make a list of ways you could improve your practice of prayer. Consider what hinders your prayer life and how those hindrances could be removed.

6. When and where do you pray? List the occasions (times) and
   locations (places).

7. Mark an X after each phrase describing an activity included in
   your prayers:

   a. Adoration and worship of God   _____

   b. Praise to God   _____

   c. Petition (asking) for your own concerns   _____

   d. Petition (asking) for the concerns of your family   _____

   e. Petition (asking) for the concerns of your friends   _____

   f. Petition (asking) for missionaries   _____

   g. Petition (asking) for church leaders   _____

   h. Petition (asking) for church members   _____

   i. Petition (asking) for government officials
      (local and national)   _____

   j. Petition (asking) for the world scene   _____

   k. Confession of your sin   _____

   l. Petition (asking) for nonphysical concerns
      (needs, desires)   _____

   m. Petition (asking) for physical concerns (needs,
      desires, wants)   _____

   n. Others   _____

8. Go back over the preceding list and identify the five activities that usually consume most of your prayer time. List these activities and assess whether you think you are emphasizing the things you should emphasize.

9. Study Matthew 6:9–13 and write down everything you see in this passage about effective prayer.

10. Study Ephesians 1:15–19; 3:14–21; 6:18–20; Philippians 1:3–6; 1:9–11; Colossians 1:3–13 and list everything you see in these passages about effective prayer.

11. What personal challenges have you reached and what changes should you make in your practice of prayer as a result of the self-analysis of these passages and your own prayer life?

12. What can you and will you do to make sure these changes will actually become a reality in your prayer life?

YOU AND YOUR BIBLE

1. How would you characterize your Bible readings or Bible study practice?

   a. Very satisfactory

   b. Satisfactory

   c. Satisfactory but needing improvement

   d. Unsatisfactory

   e. Very unsatisfactory

2. Briefly state your reasons for answering question 1 as you did.

3. On a scale from 0–10, with 10 being the highest rating, how important do you consider Bible reading or Bible study in the Christian life?   ____

4. On a scale of 0–10, how important is Bible reading or Bible study in your actual practice?   ____

5. If you think your Bible reading or Bible study practice should be improved, make a list of ways you could improve your Bible reading or Bible study. Consider what hinders your Bible reading or Bible study and how those hindrances could be removed.

6. When and where do you read or study your Bible? List the occasions (times) and locations (places).

7. Mark an X after each phrase describing a factor involved in your Bible reading or Bible study practice.

   a. Regularity   _____

   b. Memorization   _____

   c. Meditation   _____

   d. Prayer before Bible study or Bible reading   _____

   e. Personal application of what you study   _____

   f. Looking up cross-references   _____

   g. Use of commentaries   _____

   h. Writing down your thoughts in a notebook for review and preservation   _____

   i. Finding a quiet place   _____

   j. Sharing what you learned with others   _____

   k. Use of different Bible translations   _____

   l. Personalization of what you learned   _____

   m. Prayer for help to live out what you learned   _____

   n. Asking others for help when you do not understand   _____

   o. Other   _____

8. Study Joshua 1:8–9; Ezra 7:10; Psalms 1:1–3; 19:7–11; 119:1–11, 72, 82, 92, 116, 127; Proverbs 6:20–23; Isaiah 8:19–20; John 5:39–40; 17:17; Acts 17:11; Colossians 3:16; 2 Timothy 2:15; Hebrews 4:12; James 1:18–25.

   Write down everything you see in these passages about Bible reading or Bible study.

9. What personal challenges have you received and what changes should you make in your Bible reading and Bible study practice as a result of a study of these passages and your self-evaluation?

10. What can you and will you do to make sure these changes become a reality in your practice?

6

Communicating: Part 1

Preparing for marriage God's way will require you to devote your attention to your communication with each other. God is vitally concerned about this aspect of your relationship. Indeed, He says that He is grieved when there is a deficiency in this area of your life (Eph. 4:29–30).

But more than that, the depth and satisfaction of your relationship is dependent on how well you are doing in this area. You will never develop or maintain a marriage that approximates God's desires apart from an effective communication system.

In a sense, your communication may be seen as the lifeblood of the marriage relationship. In the human body if something hinders the flow of the blood, the whole person suffers. So, too, if something interferes with the flow of your communication, your whole relationship will reap the consequences.

Most marriage counselors will agree that a breakdown of communication is almost always involved in marital dysfunction. No one working in this realm disputes the fact that ineffective communication has disastrous results.

All sorts of unpleasant things may happen when people don't communicate effectively. Issues will remain unclarified. Wrong ideas will continue uncorrected. Conflicts and misunderstandings will be perpetuated. Confusion and disorder will occur. The development of deep unity, emotional closeness, and intimacy will be hindered. Interpersonal problems pile up, and barriers will become higher and wider. The temptation to look for someone else who will satisfy social desires may be encouraged. Wise decision making will be thwarted.

And these are just for starters. Without a doubt, proper communication is a key to establishing and maintaining a deep and satisfying marital relationship. Without it, you will be inhibited from developing a marriage that reflects God's beautiful plan for husbands and wives.

You may think that your communication is working quite effectively. Perhaps you are convinced that this is one area in which there is little room for improvement. Possibly you think that if it doesn't need fixing, don't fix it.

After all, you talk about everything. You share with one another freely. You are able to be lovingly honest about what you think and how you feel. You understand each other. You listen respectfully and respond appropriately. You are able to disagree and discuss your disagreements without becoming hurt or attacking one another. Your conversation is beneficial and uplifting.

Well, if these things are true of your relationship, *great!* You're very fortunate. You're laying a good foundation for a successful relationship, because effective communication is a critical factor in developing a really good marriage.

Keep on doing whatever you are doing that is right. Don't become nonchalant. Never cease working on this facet of your relationship.

My experience as a marriage and family counselor has brought me into contact with many who say, "I don't know what has happened to us. We used to be able to communicate very well. We used to talk about everything. We enjoyed sharing. We kept no secrets. We could discuss disagreements. We listened to one another. We understood each other.

"But that's all different now. We don't seem to have anything to talk about. And when we do communicate, it often ends in disaster. We just don't seem to be on the same wavelength anymore."

This scenario may illustrate two things.

First, it may indicate that these people were wrong about the way they assessed their previous communication. It may not have been as effective as they thought it was. We sometimes tend to romanticize what takes place in courtship and the early stages of marriage.

Second, this scenario may demonstrate what happens when you neglect some activity in which you had developed some expertise. This may occur by default rather than design. Almost no one deliberately decides to neglect this area. It just happens.

But whether by design or default, the consequences are still the same. The couple drifts apart. The relationship deteriorates. Emotional closeness disappears. Basic communication skills and efforts degenerate.

So, even if communication is one of your strong points, take these studies on communication seriously. Using the words of the apostle Paul out of context, excel even more (1 Thess. 4:10). Remember, there's always room for improvement.

Effective communication is so important and complex that we are devoting two sessions to it. You will be challenged to evaluate your communication system, to explore certain aspects of what God has to say about communication in His Word, and to practice the effective communication style prescribed therein.

Okay, it's time to roll up your sleeves, pray fervently, find a quiet place, pick up pen and Bible, put on your thinking cap, and go to work on the exercises.

Assignments:
1. *Assessing Your Communication*
2. *Nonverbal Communication*
3. *Communication Challenges*

ASSESSING YOUR COMMUNICATION

Do this individually. Follow the instructions carefully. Be very honest about your perspective and desires. Then get together and discuss your answers. Write down the conclusions you reached. And, as always, record any questions for discussion that this exercise generates.

1. What does it mean to be able to communicate with another person? Define what you think constitutes effective communication.

2. Consider the following items. Which ones do you communicate about? Rate the *quality* of your communication on each of these items as Excellent (E); Good (G); Fair (F); Poor (P). Rate the *quantity* of your communication on each of these items in terms of Too Much (TM); Just Right (JR); Too Little (TL); Nonexistent (N).

	Quality	Quantity
Spiritual issues, church, Christian service, devotions	___	___
Facts, information	___	___
Ideas, opinions, judgments	___	___
Desires, concerns, interests	___	___
Feelings, emotions	___	___
Plans, goals, purposes	___	___

Expectations, aspirations	_____	_____
Finances	_____	_____
Work or school	_____	_____
Family matters, parenting	_____	_____
Dreams	_____	_____
Sex	_____	_____
Friends	_____	_____
Recreation, sports	_____	_____
Problems, failures, defeats	_____	_____
Joys, victories, successes	_____	_____
Current events	_____	_____
What you read, study	_____	_____
TV or movies	_____	_____

a. List the items in which you would like to improve your communication:

b. List other items that could be included in your communication which are not listed previously:

   c. List items on which you find yourself in frequent disagreement with others. Why?

   d. Identify factors that have hindered effective communication for you and for others.

NONVERBAL COMMUNICATION

Be aware that communication is more than words. It's done by the expression on your face, the way you laugh, what you laugh at or don't laugh at, the way you use your hands or don't use your hands, the way you use your time or don't use your time, etc.

Whether you like it or not, you are communicating all the time by your nonverbal behavior. And you'd better believe that this nonverbal communication is powerful. In fact, if there's a contradiction between what people hear and what they see, they'll probably be inclined to believe what they see rather than what they hear.

So give your full attention to this assignment and learn what you can about the way you and your partner communicate. Get in touch with your own nonverbal language. Become sensitive to what signals and messages you're sending out. Recognize your nonverbal behavior's power to build or destroy. Work on eliminating destructive signals and increasing positive, enriching messages.

1. Make a list of the following Scripture references and then study (write down) what each one indicates about nonverbal communication.

   Genesis 3:7–10

   Genesis 4:5–6

   Genesis 32:6–7

   Genesis 37:3

   Genesis 39:4

   Genesis 40:6–7

Joshua 7:6

1 Samuel 1:4–10

1 Samuel 18:4

1 Kings 19:3–4a

1 Kings 21:4

Proverbs 4:25–26

Proverbs 7:6–9

Proverbs 7:10–13a

Proverbs 31:12–27

Mark 2:3–5

Luke 10:30–35a

Luke 15:3–4, 8, 20

Luke 18:10–13

1 John 3:17

2. Practice communicating at least six of the following emotions, attitudes, or issues in a nonverbal way. Do not say a word; just communicate by nonverbal means. Do not tell the other person what you are attempting to communicate. Let the other person guess. Alternate the exercise from one person to the next. Keep a record of how many times you accurately read what the other person was feeling or attempting to communicate.

Love	Anxiety	Humility
Happiness	Anger	Guilt
Peace	Sexual Interest	Disinterest
Uneasiness	Frustration	Cautiousness
Fear	Irritation	Hurt
Sadness	Discouragement	Trust
Indifference	Unbelief	Confidence
Apathy	Doubt	Pride

3. Discuss and write down what you learned from, or felt, while performing this exercise.

4. Developing oneness in marriage requires communicating properly, both verbally and nonverbally.

   a. List at least ten nonverbal ways of communicating with another person.

   b. List some nonverbal behaviors that may hinder the development of a deep and satisfying relationship in marriage.

c. List some nonverbal behaviors that may enhance oneness
    and make marriage a satisfying experience.

d. Identify the nonverbal behaviors that you do that could
    hinder oneness.

e. Identify the nonverbal behaviors that you do that encour-
    age a good relationship.

f. Discuss these items thoroughly with each other and write how you will improve your nonverbal communication.

COMMUNICATION CHALLENGES

Effects of Failed Communication

Consider what happens when people don't communicate effectively. Try to think of illustrations from your own experience, from others, or from the Bible.

1. Issues remain unclarified. (Prov. 18:17)

2. Wrong ideas or assumptions are uncorrected.

3. Conflicts remain unresolved.

4. Confusion and disorder develop.

5. Wise decision making is thwarted.

6. The development of deep unity, intimacy, and emotional closeness is hindered.

7. Interpersonal problems are intensified.

8. Boredom, discontentment, and frustration with the relationship are fostered.

9. Spiritual growth, mutual sharpening, and stimulation are impeded.

10. Shallow relationships, distancing, estrangement, and drifting apart are promoted.

11. Bad attitudes toward, suspiciousness of the other person are nurtured.

12. Understanding each other deeply is prevented.

Means of Communication

Reflect on the different means and facets of communication. Give illustrations of what and how you may communicate by these means.

1. Visually: with a wink, by staring, etc.

2. Verbally: what you say or don't say and how you say it.

3. By notes or letters.

4. By facial expressions: smiles or frowns, etc.

5. With your body: hand or feet motions, rigidity, etc.

6. By your presence or absence.

7. By a touch, a hug, a pat, a squeeze, a slap, a caress, etc.

8. By helping or not helping.

9. By giving or withholding a present.

10. By a willingness to share or an unwillingness to share.

11. By listening carefully or refusing to listen.

12. By seeking and accepting advice or by doing the opposite.

13. Other ways that you can think of:

Styles of Communication

Think about the different levels or styles of communication. Give at least one example of ways you have or could communicate on each of these levels. Assess your own and your partner's communication on each of these levels. Identify ways in which you should improve.

RATING SCALE:

2 = Very good (just right)
1 = Adequate but could stand some improvement
0+ = Inadequate (too much)
0– = Inadequate (too little)

	You	Partner
1. Cliché level: *Hello, how are you? Nice day, isn't it?*	_____	_____
2. Sharing facts or information about work, people, news events, your reading, etc.	_____	_____
3. Sharing ideas, opinions, thoughts, plans, and judgments: *I like . . . I don't like . . . I think . . . My view of this is . . . I want to . . .*	_____	_____
4. Sharing feelings or emotions: *I am really sad about . . . Right now I am very discouraged or happy or whatever . . . I am really starting to get upset or angry or (?) about what has just happened or been said.*	_____	_____
5. Asking questions, exploring, or interviewing: *What do you think about . . . ? Tell me about your day or (?). What do you really want to do? If you could do anything you wanted to do, what would it be? What has the Lord been teaching you recently? How can I improve . . . ?*	_____	_____
6. Making suggestions: *Perhaps it would be a good idea to . . . In my opinion, you're trying to do too much.*	_____	_____

7. Giving support, appreciation, affirmation, comfort, or encouragement: *I believe you can do it. Thanks, I needed or wanted that. You're doing a great job. You have been such a blessing to me. I was really helped by what you said about . . . I'm praying for you. I see God at work in your life.* ____ ____

8. Giving instruction or direction: *The Bible teaches . . . In Ephesians 4:25, God says . . . What that means is . . . You should . . .* ____ ____

9. Admonishing, correcting, confronting: *Here's an area of your thinking or life that you are neglecting. At times you seem to be very irritated. Sometimes when other people talk to you, you don't seem to be interested. When you did or said such and such, I thought or felt that you were putting me down or rejecting me.* ____ ____

10. Acknowledging sins and failures: *Please forgive me. What I did was wrong. I've asked God for forgiveness and now I'm asking you for the same. Will you forgive me? I really blew it that time. With God's help, I'll try to do better. When I did thus and such, I was very inconsiderate and insensitive.* ____ ____

11. Talking over plans and decisions. ____ ____

12. Making plans and decisions mutually. ____ ____

13. Discussing problems, disagreements, controversial issues. ____ ____

14. Praying together. ____ ____

15. Discussing Scripture, spiritual issues. ____ ____

16. Sharing the Gospel, the way God has and is blessing you. ____ ____

17. Giving praise to God. ____ ____

Causes of Communication Breakdown

Make a list of the "circuit jammers" (hindrances to good communication) found in these verses.

1. Proverbs 11:12

2. Proverbs 11:13

3. Proverbs 12:16

4. Proverbs 12:18

5. Proverbs 15:1

6. Proverbs 15:5

7. Proverbs 16:27

8. Proverbs 17:9

9. Proverbs 18:2

10. Proverbs 18:6

11. Proverbs 18:8

12. Proverbs 18:13

13. Proverbs 18:17

14. Proverbs 18:23

15. Proverbs 19:1

16. Proverbs 19:5

17. Proverbs 20:19

18. Proverbs 20:25

19. Proverbs 25:24

20. Proverbs 26:18–19

21. Proverbs 26:20–21

22. Proverbs 26:22

23. Proverbs 27:2

24. Proverbs 29:20

25. Ephesians 4:25

26. Ephesians 4:29

27. Ephesians 4:31

28. Colossians 3:8

29. Colossians 3:9

Rating Your Communication: Part 1

Review the list of hindrances to good communication you noted in the previous section. Evaluate yourself and your partner on each of the items on this list to discern what you are doing well and how you need to improve, writing down your rating beside each verse. Be honest about your ratings. Make this exercise a real learning experience. The higher your scores, the better will be your communication and your relationship.

RATING SCALE:
4 = Never do this
3 = Seldom do this
2 = Sometimes do this
1 = Frequently do this
0 = Always do this

Make a list of any of the hindrances on which you or your partner rated you 0, 1, or 2. Think about, pray about, discuss, and plan what you can do to improve.

What Not to Say

Another important aspect of proper communication is knowing what to avoid in terms of what you actually say. Scripture has a lot to say about the way you use your tongue. The Lord is quite clear about the wrong way to speak to and about one another. It is therefore important to understand what God has to say about the wrong way of using your tongue. Now complete the worksheet to help you identify and eliminate any destructive speech patterns that you may be practicing.

Read the following sentences and determine which of the principles listed under Causes of Communication Breakdown they violate. Which circuit jammers do they illustrate?

1. You make me sick. _____

2. I hope you get what you deserve. _____

3. If you don't like it, you can lump it. _____

4. You never do a good job at anything you do. _____

5. I don't really care what you think. _____

6. You're going to be sorry. _____

7. I can't promise you what I'm going to do. _____

8. You are such a nitwit, a real nincompoop. _____

9. Why don't you just shut up! _____

10. Whatever I set my mind to, I can do. _____

11. This time I'm going to get even. _____

12. I'm going to teach you a real lesson. _____

13. Drop dead! _____

14. Let me tell you how it is. _____

15. Just be quiet and let me tell you what you should do. I don't need to hear anymore. _____

16. Why in the world would you ever do something like that! _____

17. If you were a real woman or man, you . . . _____

18. I know I promised to do it, but . . . _____

19. You're making a big deal out of nothing. _____

20. Anybody knows it's not the way you say it is. _____

21. After what you've done, you expect me to love you? _____

22. Let me tell you about what so and so did. _____

23. I've talked to you about this a million times. _____

24. Here we go again! _____

25. I don't want to hear about your problems. I've got enough of my own. _____

26. You don't care at all about what I think. _____

27. I know you said _____ but this is what's really happening. _____

28. No one else understands it or can do it as well as I. _____

29. You're never satisfied. You're the one who is causing problems. _____

30. It's all your fault. _____

31. Why don't you get off your high horse! _____

32. So I lied. Don't make such a big deal out of it. _____

33. You should have known I didn't really mean it. Anybody knows I was only kidding. You just take things too seriously. _____

Rating Your Communication: Part 2

Go back over this list and put a circle around the number of any of the statements that are similar to ones that you have made. Put a check mark in front of the statements that are similar to ones that you have heard your partner make. Discuss the impact of such statements on you, your relationship, and others. Pray and work on eliminating such statements from your conversation.

7

Communicating: Part 2

*I*n session 6, you explored the key issues of nonverbal communication and communication hindrances. In this session, you will be discussing two more important aspects.

Now that you have seen what to avoid (the circuit jammers), it will be meaningful to explore what Scripture has to say about what helps or promotes good communication.

Good listening is an important part of effective communication. Talking is not necessarily the same as communicating. Talking involves sending a message. Communicating includes accurately *receiving* the message as well. It involves people coming to a common meaning so that both sender and receiver are drawn together and mutually enriched and encouraged (Eph. 4:25, 29).

For this to occur, there must be good listening and good speaking. Scripture has much to say about the foolishness of answering a matter before we have listened. Yet often we are so busy talking or planning how to respond that we don't really listen to the other person. As a result, we don't communicate effectively and we don't relate deeply.

Assignments:

1. *Effective Communication*

2. *Suggestions for Good Marital Communication*

3. *Are You Listening?*
4. *Communication Checklist*

Additional study:
For further help with communication or conflict resolution, see Wayne Mack's book *Your Family, God's Way* (Phillipsburg, P&R Publishing, 1991).

EFFECTIVE COMMUNICATION

1. Make a list of things that you can share with your partner.

2. Make a list of helps to good communication found in the following verses.

   Psalm 141:3

   Proverbs 5:18–19

Proverbs 12:25

Proverbs 15:1

Proverbs 15:2

Proverbs 15:28

Proverbs 16:23–24

Proverbs 17:14

Proverbs 18:23

Proverbs 20:5

Proverbs 20:15

Proverbs 25:9

Proverbs 25:11–12

Proverbs 25:15

Proverbs 29:11

Proverbs 31:26

Ecclesiastes 12:10

Isaiah 8:10, 20

Isaiah 50:4

Matthew 19:3–4

Romans 13:7–8

Galatians 5:13

Ephesians 4:15, 25

Ephesians 4:26–27

Ephesians 4:29

Ephesians 4:32

Ephesians 5:33

1 Peter 3:1–7

3. List at least ten important communication enhancers, promoters, or facilitators that you found in these verses.

4. List three times or situations when you did not communicate well. Using the guidelines from the previous verses, analyze these incidents to discern what you could have done that would have been more effective.

5. Using the following list as headings, list three items under each in order of priority as you believe your partner would respond: his or her joys; disappointments; goals; dislikes; interests; concerns. Ask your partner to check your knowledge of him or her.

    a. Joys

b. Disappointments

c. Goals

d. Dislikes

  e. Interests

  f. Concerns

6. Make a list of at least ten fun things your partner enjoys that you can enjoy together. Plan to do at least one each week.

7. List the personal insights and challenges you have received from this study. Be personal and specific.

SUGGESTIONS FOR GOOD MARITAL COMMUNICATION

RATING SCALE:
4 = Always
3 = Often
2 = Sometimes
1 = Seldom
0 = Never

	You	Partner
1. When there are problems, each must be willing to admit that he or she is part of the problem. (Gen. 3:8–19; Prov. 20:6)	____	____
2. Each person must be willing to change. (Matt. 5:23–26; John 5:6)	____	____
3. Avoid the use of emotionally charged words. "You don't really love me." "You always do . . ." "You never do anything right." "I don't care."	____	____
4. Be responsible for your own emotions, words, actions, and reactions. Don't blame them on the other person. You got angry, lashed out, became depressed, etc. (Gal. 6:5; James 1:13–15)	____	____
5. Refrain from having reruns of old arguments. (Eph. 4:26)	____	____
6. Deal with one problem at a time. Solve one problem and then move on to the next. (Matthew 6:34 principle)	____	____
7. Deal in the present and not in the past. Hang a "no fishing" sign over the past unless it will help you to solve your present problems. (Isa. 43:25; Jer. 31:34; Phil. 3:12–14)	____	____
8. Major on the positive instead of majoring on the negative. (Phil. 4:8)	____	____

9. Learn to communicate in nonverbal ways. (Ps. 32:8; Matt. 8:1–2, 14–15)   ____   ____

10. Express your thoughts and concerns to each other. Relate your activities. Listen, understand, and respond to the meaning behind what a person is saying. When he flies off the handle at you, he may be saying, "I've had a terrible day at the job. Nobody respects me." When she says, "You don't love me," she may be really saying, "I desperately need some affection. I'm starved for love." (Example of Jesus in Mark 5:1–15; John 1:45–47; 11:20–35)   ____   ____

11. Practice the golden rule (Matt. 7:12). What would you like your spouse to do to you? Would you like your spouse to tell you the truth? Ask your opinion? Help in time of need? Be natural around you? Thank you for your help or services? Well, then do the same for him or her.   ____   ____

12. Practice the principle laid down in Luke 6:35: "Do good, and lend, expecting nothing in return."   ____   ____

ARE YOU LISTENING?

Listening well is a very important part of effective communication and an essential element in developing deep, godly relationships. To discover your "listening quotient" (i.e., how well you are doing as a listener), complete the following inventory and then ask a close friend who will give you honest feedback to do the same. Write down the appropriate number representing your listening behavior for each statement.

RATING SCALE:
3 = Usually
2 = Sometimes
1 = Seldom
0 = Never

1. I realize that listening is an important aspect of ministering to another person. _____

2. When someone else is speaking to me, I pay close attention to that person and don't allow my mind to wander. _____

3. I don't close my mind to what the other person is saying even if it differs with my own ideas; I am willing to learn and evaluate what I hear; and I speak biblically. _____

4. I don't stop listening to the other person even if he or she is saying something I don't want to hear. _____

5. People who know me would say I am a good listener. _____

6. I refrain from judging what the other person has said until I'm sure I have understood what he or she means; I do not jump to conclusions. _____

7. I realize the other person knows what he or she meant better than I do. _____

8. I refrain from predicting what the other person is going to say. _____

9. I refuse to use the time when the other person is speaking to prepare my rebuttal; I concentrate on trying to understand what the other person is saying, feeling, and thinking rather than on my response to what is being said.   _____

10. I'm willing to be rebuked, criticized, or challenged without defending myself or immediately and excessively explaining myself.   _____

11. I withhold glib and hasty advice.   _____

12. I refrain from apologizing too quickly to get the other person to stop talking, resulting in his or her thinking I am not sincere and I really do not understand his or her feelings.   _____

13. I'm slow to correct the other person's evaluation of an issue.   _____

14. I hesitate to tell the other person how he or she should or should not feel about a matter.   _____

15. When someone else has spoken, I can accurately summarize and reflect what has been said.   _____

16. When another person is speaking, I refuse to interrupt; I am a patient listener.   _____

17. When someone else is speaking, I listen with my whole being (eyes, mind, ears, hands, feet, body posture, thoughts, inner man, and outer man).   _____

Study the following verses and write down what each of them has to say about listening, hearing, paying attention, being quiet:

1. Genesis 21:17–18

2. Exodus 2:23–24

3. Exodus 22:25–27

4. Job 21:1–2

5. Job 31:35

6. Psalm 6:3–9

7. Proverbs 1:5, 8, 33

8. Proverbs 2:1–2

9. Proverbs 4:1, 10, 20

10. Proverbs 5:1–2

11. Proverbs 8:6–7, 32–33

12. Proverbs 10:8, 14

13. Proverbs 12:15

14. Proverbs 13:1

15. Proverbs 15:31

16. Proverbs 17:1, 4

17. Proverbs 18:2, 13, 15

18. Proverbs 19:20, 27

19. Proverbs 25:12

20. Proverbs 29:20

21. Isaiah 30:15; 32:17

22. Amos 5:13

23. John 11:41–42

24. 1 Thessalonians 4:11–12

25. 1 Timothy 2:2

26. James 1:19

27. 1 Peter 3:4

Apply what you have learned in this inventory and Bible study by completing the following statements:

1. By God's grace I am a good listener in these ways:

2. With God's help I need to work on improving my listening skills in these ways and areas:

3. To improve my listening skills, I will:

COMMUNICATION CHECKLIST*

Rate both yourself and your partner on a scale of 1–5 on each of the following qualities of biblical communication.

RATING SCALE:
5 = Excellent
4 = Good
3 = Fair
2 = Weak
1 = Very weak

	You	Partner
1. Does not lie. (Prov. 12:19; Eph. 4:25)	____	____
2. Is not evasive, but willing to share everything. (Eph. 4:25)	____	____
3. Never flatters.	____	____
4. Speaks and does not clam up when under pressure or attack. (Eph. 4:25)	____	____
5. Lets someone know in a controlled way why he or she is angry with that person. (Eph. 4:26)	____	____
6. If bothered by someone, immediately finds time to discuss it with the offending party.	____	____
7. Is able to constructively discuss a problem he or she is angry about.	____	____
8. Does not say anything in an unloving way to someone who may be wrong.	____	____
9. Does not say anything in a disrespectful way to someone who may be wrong.	____	____
10. Does not use God's name in frustration, bitterness, rage, or irritation. (Eph. 4:29)	____	____

* Used by permission of Rev. James Petty.

11. Does not say things to hurt others or make another feel bad. (Eph. 4:29)   ____ ____

12. Says things in a way calculated to help the other person understand that he or she did wrong and gives the person hope for improvement.   ____ ____

13. Only says things that help in a conflict situation, not things that make it worse.   ____ ____

14. Always conditions criticism with some note of appreciation for legitimate strengths.   ____ ____

15. Does not react emotionally when verbally ignored, attacked, frustrated, etc. (Prov. 15:1; Eph. 4:31–32)   ____ ____

16. Acts to diffuse conflict situations by a kind word or inquiry, in a spirit of reconciliation. (Prov. 15:1)   ____ ____

17. Communicates with God in prayer every day.   ____ ____

18. Communicates honestly with God.   ____ ____

19. Shares significant events and concerns each day with partner to the extent he or she desires to hear those things.   ____ ____

20. Desires to pray each day with partner about common concerns, praises.   ____ ____

21. Spends time with God, focusing on listening to God's Word in the Scriptures.   ____ ____

22. Is able to speak God's Word in a situation in such a way that it produces encouragement, hope, and greater strength. (Prov. 12:18, 25; Isa. 50:4)   ____ ____

23. Thinks carefully before speaking in tense situations. (Prov. 15:28; 16:23; 29:20)   ____ ____

24. Is able to diffuse an argument by graciously dropping a matter when it is producing a quarrel. (Prov. 17:4)   ____ ____

25. Does not answer harshly to those over whom he or she has power. (Prov. 18:23)   ____   ____

26. Is able and willing to draw out the feelings and thoughts of others close to him or her. (Prov. 20:5; 1 Peter 3:7)   ____   ____

27. Only speaks when well informed or knowledgeable about what should be said. (Prov. 20:15; 18:2)   ____   ____

28. Does not speak about people in a way that betrays confidence or belittles them before others. (Prov. 25:9; 11:13; 17:9; 18:8; 26:22)   ____   ____

29. Is able to rebuke others when needed. (Prov. 25:12; Rom. 15:14)   ____   ____

30. Is able and willing to communicate the gospel or other Scripture as needed. (Prov. 31:26)   ____   ____

31. Speaks respectfully about and to those in authority. (Rom. 13:7)   ____   ____

32. Often includes words of delight and appreciation in conversations concerning his or her partner.   ____   ____

33. Listens carefully and attentively when rebuked or criticized. (Prov. 15:5; 18:13)   ____   ____

34. Keeps verbal promises. (Prov. 20:25; 26:18–19)   ____   ____

35. Knows when and how to bring up a disagreement so that a contentious spirit is not projected. (Prov. 25:24; 26:21)   ____   ____

36. Does not hurt people in jest.   ____   ____

37. Usually speaks in a way that others respect. (Prov. 28:2)   ____   ____

38. Is never afraid to speak up to those who disagree and to take a stand when important issues are at stake.   ____   ____

8

Resolving Conflicts

*O*ne thing is for sure—a Christian home is not a home without problems and conflicts. In his commentary on Matthew 18:15, John Trapp says it is as unlikely that you could strike two pieces of flint together and not have sparks as it is that you could put two sinners together and not have conflicts.*

The truth is that whenever two people enter into a really close relationship, some disagreements are inevitable. They are bound to occur.

Probably the two of you already know that from personal experience in your relationship. If you don't, you will. You will have differences of opinion on certain issues, or else one of you doesn't do any thinking.

Disagreements are not necessarily bad. If there are not too many of them, they can be very helpful. If they are faced and handled God's way, they can have a positive impact rather than a negative one.

In fact, many couples who respond to their differences in a biblical way often find that these disagreements stimulate growth and development in their lives and relationship. Contrasting or diverse viewpoints at first may appear to be monsters to be greatly feared. Later, when confronted and handled God's way, they turn out to be friends in disguise.

In this session, you'll see that God says conflicts may be resolved when people are willing to deal with them His way. You'll also note that God is very realistic in terms of what He *doesn't say* about conflict resolution.

Nowhere does the Bible indicate that conflict resolution comes naturally. For some reason, it's often easier to fight and argue than to

---

* John Trapp, "Commentary on Matthew 18," *John Trapp Complete Commentary*, StudyLight.org, accessed September 3, 2013, http://www.studylight.org/com/jtc/view.cgi?bk=39&ch=18.

want to be a peacemaker. It's often more natural to provoke and prolong than to pacify contention. When disagreements arise, how inclined we are to bite and devour rather than love (Gal. 5:13–16).

God doesn't suggest that resolving conflicts is a piece of cake. Rather, He acknowledges that it's sometimes very difficult to come to agreement (Prov. 18:19). It often requires a lot of work and effort. Though conflict resolution may be difficult, God makes it clear that with His help it isn't impossible. It doesn't come easily, but it can come if you will carefully follow His directives.

Fortunately, God's directives for resolving conflicts are given in abundant fashion in His Word. In this area, you don't need to thrash around on your own trying to find the best way to deal with the situation. It's not necessary for you to depend upon the fallible and often conflicting views of men. You can turn to God's infallible Word and discover His practical conflict resolution guidelines. And you can be assured that if anything will work, they will.

In this session, you will be exposed to some of these directives. Take them seriously. Do the assignments carefully. One day, perhaps today, you'll be glad you did.

Now seek God's help in prayer, find a quiet place, pick up Bible and pen, put on your thinking cap, and go to work on the following assignments. Afterward, write a one or two page summary of your responses to the assignments: what you have learned about yourself, your partner, and your relationship; how you were challenged; areas in which you need to improve and areas in which you are doing well; questions you would like to ask; issues about conflict resolution or other matters you would like to discuss.

Assignments:

1. *How to Avoid Strife and Contention.* Select at least fifteen verses to study at this time; if you choose, you may look up the other verses at another time.

2. *Good Conflict Resolution*

3. *Conflict Analysis*

4. *Problem Solving*

5. *Sorting Out Responsibilities Checklist*

Additional study:

For further help with communication or conflict resolution, see Wayne Mack's book *Your Family, God's Way* (Phillipsburg, P&R Publishing, 1991).

HOW TO AVOID STRIFE AND CONTENTION

Ask God for help. (Matt. 7:7–9; James 4:2–3)

Genesis 13:8–9	Proverbs 20:3
Genesis 26:17–31	Proverbs 21:9, 19
Judges 8:1–3	Proverbs 25:8
Judges 12:1–3	Proverbs 26:17, 21
2 Samuel 10:1–14	Proverbs 29:20, 22
2 Samuel 19:41–43	Ecclesiastes 10:4
2 Kings 14:1–8	Jeremiah 28:1–11
Proverbs 10:12	Daniel 1:8–16
Proverbs 13:10	Romans 12:14–21
Proverbs 15:1, 4, 18	Romans 13:12–14
Proverbs 16:32	Colossians 3:12–15
Proverbs 17:14, 27	1 Timothy 6:1–4
Proverbs 18:6, 19	James 3:14–4:2
Proverbs 19:11, 13	James 4:2

Carefully study at least fifteen of the passages above and write down everything you see in them about strife, fighting, quarreling, and contention. Look at each passage and identify, if you can:

1. Why people fight and/or quarrel.

2. What it says about why you get into quarrels.

3. What it says about a person who quarrels and/or fights and what it calls that person.

4. The consequences of quarreling and/or fighting.

5. What must be done to restrain and overcome strife and contention (be specific).

Choose several verses to memorize. Write them on 3 x 5 cards and work on memorizing them.

Select three times when you were involved in a strife situation and, using the information from your Bible study on strife, analyze and:

   1. Write what you did that was biblical.

   2. Write the ways in which you erred.

3. Write what you could have done differently.

4. Imagine (picture) yourself actually following biblical directions in the situation.

5. Pray about the situation (confess sin, ask for specific help, thank God that He will give it).

Keep a daily conflict or strife journal.

1. Record the facts—what happened, what was said and done, how you felt, what was the outcome.

2. Analyze what you did or said that was biblical and/or unbiblical.

3. Write out other things you could have done that would have been in harmony with Scripture.

GOOD CONFLICT RESOLUTION

This exercise will help you discern the kind of marriage partners the two of you may be. It is a list of what you and your partner should be doing when you have disagreements.

Read each statement. Then, on the blank lines, record the number that corresponds to how often you and your partner practice this rule for effective conflict resolution.

RATING SCALE:
4 = I never do this
3 = I seldom do this
2 = I sometimes do this
1 = I frequently do this
0 = I always do this

You   Partner

1. When a disagreement or problem arises, I focus on what is happening and what I should do to correct it instead of trying to understand what my partner does.   ____   ____

2. When a problem arises, I am ready to admit that I may be part of the problem. I focus on what I am doing wrong, rather than on what my partner is doing wrong.   ____   ____

3. I realize I cannot change my partner; he or she must want to change or all my efforts will compound the problem rather than solve the problem.   ____   ____

4. I realize that love is not primarily a feeling, but actions calculated to serve, please, and help my partner in a God-honoring way.   ____   ____

5. I focus my attention on changing my own behavior, attitudes, reactions, and responses toward my partner. I plan specific, attainable, repeatable, positive changes I can make.   ____   ____

6. I am constantly working to develop and maintain a good communication system. I know that relationships are hindered when there is no communication or the wrong kind of communication.   ____   ____

7. I am working to develop and maintain many commonalities with my partner, including common projects, common interests, and common recreational activities. I do a variety of activities with him or her. I am creative in the expression of my love and appreciation of him or her.   ____   ____

8. I recognize and allow for differences between my partner and me. I know men and women tend to view things differently.   ____   ____

9. I regularly practice the Golden Rule as stated in Matthew 7:12. I treat my partner as I want to be treated.   ____   ____

10. I major on the positive qualities of my partner and our relationship rather than focus on the negative. I emphasize our commonalities rather than our differences. (Phil. 4:8)   ____   ____

11. I practice the principle laid down in Luke 6:34–35. I give and serve, expecting nothing in return.   ____   ____

12. I keep current. I deal with one problem at a time. I don't continue to have reruns of arguments from the past. I forgive and forget. (Matt. 6:34; Eph. 4:26) ____ ____

13. I try to maintain a close relationship with God through Jesus Christ. (Matt. 22:37–39; John 14:6; Eph. 5:21–33; 1 John 4:21). ____ ____

After you finish this exercise, count the number of 0 and 1 answers you gave and mark the number on the appropriate line below. Next, count the number of 2, 3, or 4 answers you gave. Record that number on the appropriate line below.

                                                            You   Partner

Number of 0 and 1 answers   ____   ____

Number of 2, 3, and 4 answers   ____   ____

This exercise describes thirteen principles for good conflict resolution in your relationship with your partner and in your dealings with other people. It describes how you can be the kind of marriage partner God wants you to be. If you honestly answered several of the statements with a 2, 3, or 4, plan how you can change in order to answer those statements with a 0 or a 1. The more 0s and 1s you have, the better will be your relationship with your partner and with others. If you are behaving one way toward your partner and another way with others, chances are that after you are married, you will begin to treat your spouse the way you treat others.

CONFLICT ANALYSIS

Most couples have disagreements and conflicts in their relationships. Indicate below the approximate extent of agreement or disagreement there is between you and your partner for each item in the list.

RATING SCALE:
6 = Always disagree
5 = Almost always disagree
4 = Frequently disagree
3 = Occasionally agree
2 = Frequently agree
1 = Always agree

Circle the numbers of the items that are sources of great trouble or serious concern for you.

1. Use of money. _____

2. Recreational matters. _____

3. Spiritual matters. _____

4. Friends (social life). _____

5. Demonstrations of affection. _____

6. Correct or proper behavior. _____

7. Philosophy of life. Goals in life. _____

8. Time spent together. _____

9. Making major decisions. _____

10. Leisure time, interests, and activities. _____

11. Career decisions. _____

12. Praying and studying the Bible together. _____

13. Where we will live after we are married. _____

14. What type of housing we will live in and our ideas of what type of housing we will want in the future. _____

15. Ways of dealing with parents and future in-laws.   _____

16. Use of alcohol or drugs.   _____

17. How to resolve disagreements.   _____

On a scale from 0–10 (0 = lowest; 10 = highest), indicate your overall satisfaction level with your present relationship.   _____

PROBLEM SOLVING

List below the solutions to at least five problems that you have solved together God's way. These should be problems where you have had differences of opinion, difficult decisions to make, arguments, or personal antagonisms to overcome.

   Problem One:

 1. Define clearly.

 2. What does the Bible say about the problem?

 3. Determine practical ways for implementing biblical principles in solving this problem.

Problem Two:

1. Define clearly.

2. What does the Bible say about the problem?

3. Determine practical ways for implementing biblical principles in solving this problem.

Problem Three:

1. Define clearly.

2. What does the Bible say about the problem?

3. Determine practical ways for implementing biblical principles in solving this problem.

Problem Four:

1. Define clearly.

2. What does the Bible say about the problem?

3. Determine practical ways for implementing biblical principles in solving this problem.

Problem Five:

1. Define clearly.

2. What does the Bible say about the problem?

3. Determine practical ways for implementing biblical principles in solving this problem.

SORTING OUT RESPONSIBILITIES

A Plan for Promoting Unity in Marriage and Overcoming Marital Conflicts

Many times conflicts arise in marriage because there has been no clear delineation of responsibilities. Sometimes when everything is everybody's responsibility, everything becomes nobody's responsibility. Or everybody is trying to do the same thing, and confusion, frustration, bitterness, and competitiveness are the result. One person has one view about how or when something should be done, and the other person has another, and neither is willing to yield. Or one person always seems to do the yielding. This provides the soil in which sinful and unnecessary resentment and bitterness may develop.

Much of this conflict can be eliminated if clear lines of responsibility are delineated. The husband under God is the head or manager of the home (Eph. 5:22–27; 1 Tim. 3:4–5). He is the one who is finally responsible to lovingly and biblically guide the home. The buck stops with him. But he may decide to let his wife (his chief helper—Gen. 2:18; Prov. 31:10–31) take the leadership responsibility in certain areas. Indeed, he will be wise to do this because she most certainly has more gifts, abilities, insight, and experience in some areas than he does. In other areas, he will be more gifted and capable than she, and there he should take the lead in making decisions.

The husband and wife should share insights and advice in every area, but someone ought to be given the responsibility of seeing that things get done. Look over the following list and decide who will have the responsibility to plan and implement the different areas. Remember, some things are not right or wrong—just different ways of doing things or different ways of looking at something. In areas that are not vitally important or clearly spelled out in Scripture, be willing to defer to the other person. Don't make mountains out of molehills! Don't make everything a major issue! Talk matters over, assign responsibilities, make decisions, support each other, help carry out decisions.

This sorting out of responsibilities does not mean that a given area is one person's exclusive responsibility. It means that when a difference of opinion arises, one person has authority to make the choice. Certainly, in most areas a full and frank discussion will be conducted, all options and alternatives, pros and cons considered. However, when a conflict of opinion arises, someone must be allowed to make the decision, even if that decision is to wait until God brings the two of you into agreement: "If a house is divided against itself, that house will not be able to stand" (Mark 3:25).

In making a decision, make sure that you do not violate a biblical principle. Seek the opinion and insight of your spouse, ask God in prayer to guide you, believe that He will, consider and evaluate all options, and then, if you are the person who is responsible, make the decision. The other person should support the decision wholeheartedly and seek to make the decision a success unless it clearly violates biblical principles. Unity in marriage (Gen. 2:24) is tremendously important and should be maintained carefully. Following this plan is one way of promoting this unity. However, it will work only if both people agree to abide by it.

This "sorting out of responsibilities" does not mean the husband relinquishes his biblical responsibility to be the loving leader of the family. What it does mean is that he recognizes that God has given his wife certain abilities and capacities that may make her more competent in some areas than he is. Thus he delegates to her responsibilities that are in keeping with her resources. All the while, he maintains veto power, but he will not use it unless his wife's decisions clearly violate biblical principles.

Scripture declares: "[Love] is not rude; it is not self seeking" (1 Cor. 13:5 NIV). "Make my joy complete by being like minded, having the same love, being one in spirit and purpose. Do nothing out of selfish ambition or vain conceit, but in humility consider others better than yourselves. Each of you should look not only to your own interests, but also to the interests of others" (Phil. 2:2–4 NIV). "Live in harmony with one another. Don't be proud, but be willing to associate with people of low position. Do not be conceited" (Rom. 12:16 NIV). "Be devoted to one another in brotherly love. Honor one another above yourselves" (Rom. 12:10 NIV). "If you keep on biting and devouring each other . . . you will be destroyed by each other" (Gal. 5:15 NIV). "You, my brothers, were called to be free. But do not use your freedom to indulge your sinful nature; rather serve one another in love" (Gal. 5: 12 NIV).

This "Sorting Out Responsibilities" plan is offered as a means of actualizing these Bible admonitions.

SORTING OUT RESPONSIBILITIES CHECKLIST

On the lines following the descriptive phrase, indicate who will be mainly responsible for the area described:

1. Children:

   Neatness _____

   Rules and regulations _____

   Bedtimes _____

   Activities _____

   Discipline _____

   Social life (friends, dating) _____

   Clothing _____

   Allowances (money management) _____

   Chores _____

   Manners _____

   Schoolwork _____

   TV watching _____

   Hygiene _____

   Spiritual life _____

   Other (_____) _____

   Other (_____) _____

2. Money management (establishing budget) _____

3. Financing and bookkeeping (paying bills, keeping records) _____

4. Money raising _____

5. Purchasing food and household supplies _____

6. Menu planning and cooking (dietician and chef) _____

7. Housecleaning _____

8. Spiritual oversight (church selection, attendance, family goals, family devotions, etc.) _____

9. Family activities (fun times, recreation, family projects, supervision of family nights) _____

10. Vacation plans _____

11. Clothing purchasing _____

12. Clothing maintenance _____

13. Automobile (selection, maintenance, etc.) _____

14. Savings account _____

15. Hospitality (friends in for dinner, etc.) _____

16. Investment planning _____

17. Real estate purchases (home selection, etc.) _____

18. Gift planning and purchasing _____

19. Memorabilia keeping (family records, pictures, newspaper clippings, letters, etc.) _____

20. Family photography _____

21. Special events (birthdays, anniversaries, etc.) _____

22. Furniture (selection, purchases, and maintaining) _____

23. Time and schedule organizing _____

24. Travel (motel, maps, directions, etc.) _____

25. Retirement (plans and provisions) _____

26. Yard work _____

27. Gardening _____

28. Family health services _____

29. Occupation, career _____

Add any other responsibilities you can think of, under 30–32.

30. _____ _____

31. _____ _____

32. _____ _____

9

Being a Husband

$\mathcal{E}$veryone marries with certain ideas or expectations about many different issues in marriage. If the husband and wife have the same perspectives, harmony and bliss may occur. On the other hand, if their concepts are different and strongly held, division and misery may result.

People make at least three mistakes in their marital concepts and expectations. (1) Before marriage, a couple often assumes that they agree on various issues and thus never discuss them in detail. (2) They know that they have some disagreements but think they aren't important. (Actually, they don't even know how much they disagree, nor can they resolve their differences because they have never talked about them.) (3) They pretend they are in agreement with the other person when in reality they are not.

Thus they deceive themselves and others by refusing to admit what they really think. They are so intent on preventing any disturbances in their relationship that they portray a pseudo-mutuality.

On the surface, they give the impression that they agree completely, but in reality, mutuality does not exist. Sooner or later, in one way or another, under the real-life situation in marriage, they are forced to be honest. At some time after the wedding day, reality forces itself upon them.

When their hopes are not fulfilled, each of them experiences disappointment because the other person has let them down. Or they are saddened and frustrated because demands are being made of them that they perceive as unreasonable and excessive.

As has already been suggested in previous sessions, it is crucial that you and your partner explore the issue of husband/wife expectations thoroughly and come to some agreement on these matters. Sessions 8 and 9 will bring about discussion and agreement about crucial issues in your relationship.

In fulfilling the assignments in these chapters, you will be given a chance to:

- Search out your own ideas concerning the roles and responsibilities of husbands and wives in marriage.

- Come to a fuller understanding of what your partner thinks about this subject.

- Search the Scriptures to get a fuller knowledge of what God says about these issues.

- Compare and adjust your own expectations to God's good, perfect, and well-pleasing directives.

- Discuss all these important concepts thoroughly.

So roll up your sleeves, pray fervently for God's help, find a quiet place, pick up Bible and pen, put on your thinking cap, and go to work on the following assignments.

(If there is anything that you do not understand or with which you are not in agreement, write it down and bring it with you to counseling or the class session. Talk it over in the session with your counselor or teacher.)

Assignments:

1. *The Ideal Husband.* You and your partner each write a brief article built on the phrases: "An ideal husband is . . ." and "In marriage, I think the husband should . . ." In the article, be specific, practical, clear, concrete, and as thorough as possible. Study Genesis 2:18; Proverbs 31:10–31; Ephesians 5:25–33; 1 Timothy 3:4–5; 5:8; and 1 Peter 3:7–8 as you formulate your articles. Now share your "ideal husband" assignments with each other, comparing what you have written. Discuss all similarities and differences. What would you add, subtract, change, expand, or correct to make what you wrote more biblical and useful?

2. *Scorecard for Future Husbands.* Note that there is one form for the husband-to-be and another for the wife-to-be. Discuss your evaluations with each other.

3. *Interview.* Get together with a godly, successful husband and interview him about being a husband. Ask him questions such as: What are a godly husband's responsibilities to his wife? What does the Bible mean when it says that the husband is the head of the wife? What is involved in being the manager of the home? How can you know and fulfill your wife's needs? How can you develop a deep friendship with your wife? How can a husband provide leadership without demeaning or quenching his wife's initiative and creativity? What are the most important factors in being a good husband? How can a husband help his wife to grow in her God-given potential?

SCORECARD FOR FUTURE HUSBANDS (HIS)

Use this inventory to evaluate yourself as a potential husband. This inventory enumerates issues that are important factors in a good husband/wife relationship. If you are going to be the kind of husband God wants you to be, the factors that will make you that kind of husband will be evident in your life right now. On those statements where you score high (4 or 3), praise God and make sure you keep on doing these things. On those items where your score is 2 or lower, accept the challenge and work on improving.

RATING SCALE:
4 = Regularly
3 = Frequently
2 = Sometimes
1 = Rarely
0 = Never

1. I plan my time so that I can spend time with my partner. _____

2. I am courteous to her and treat her with respect. _____

3. I listen to her suggestions, advice, and even complaints without ignoring them, being threatened, or resenting the fact that she gave them. _____

4. I communicate with her, telling her what I am doing, where I am going, what my daily schedule involves. _____

5. I am on time for dates and call her if an emergency arises that will make me late. _____

6. I help my partner with her responsibilities. _____

7. I make time for the two of us to be alone together. _____

8. I refrain from shouting at her, abusing her, talking harshly or unkindly to her, or making unreasonable demands on her. _____

9. I refrain from using force (physical or psychological) to get my own way. _____

10. I avoid talking to her about women in a way that implies she is inferior. _____

11. I am willing to work hard enough to adequately provide for household and personal expenses. _____

12. I work on keeping myself physically attractive. _____

13. I seek her counsel and advice. _____

14. I look for positive qualities and behavior and enthusiastically commend her. _____

15. I show respect and esteem for her when around people; I am courteous and mannerly with her. _____

16. I avoid being a nitpicker, making mountains out of molehills. _____

17. I love sharing my ideas, interests, and life with her. _____

18. I listen to her even when she is telling me something in which I am not particularly interested. _____

19. I am a fun person to be with; I take life and myself seriously, but not too seriously. _____

20. I try to change any habits that are annoying to her. _____

21. I try to see things from her perspective and am interested in her viewpoints. _____

22. I try to love her in the way she wants to be loved. _____

23. I exercise spiritual leadership, setting an example of servanthood, leading in devotions, praying regularly for and with her. _____

24. I am sensitive to her problems and difficulties and try to be an encouragement to her. _____

25. I act like she is the most important person in my life next to the Lord; I treat her like she is really valuable; I communicate appreciation. _____

Go back over this list and make a list of all items that were scored 2, 1, or 0. Pray, think about, discuss, and plan how to make improvements on these items.

SCORECARD FOR FUTURE HUSBANDS (HERS)

Use this inventory to evaluate your future husband. This inventory enumerates issues that are important in a good husband/wife relationship. Your honest assessment can be a helpful tool in preparing for marriage God's way.

RATING SCALE:
4 = Regularly
3 = Frequently
2 = Sometimes
1 = Rarely
0 = Never

1. He plans his time so that he can spend time with me.　____
2. He is courteous to me and treats me with respect.　____
3. He listens to my suggestions, advice and even complaints without ignoring them, being threatened, or resenting the fact that I gave them.　____
4. He communicates with me, telling me what he is doing, where he is going, what his daily schedule involves.　____
5. He is on time for dates and calls me if an emergency arises that will make him late.　____
6. He helps me with my responsibilities.　____
7. He makes time for the two of us to be alone together.　____
8. He refrains from shouting at me, abusing me, talking harshly or unkindly to me, or making unreasonable demands on me.　____
9. He refrains from using force (physical or psychological) to get his own way.　____
10. He avoids talking to me about women in a way that implies I am inferior.　____
11. He is willing to work hard enough to adequately provide for household and personal expenses.　____
12. He works on keeping himself physically attractive.　____

13. He seeks my counsel and advice. _____

14. He looks for positive qualities and behavior and enthusiastically commends me. _____

15. He shows respect and esteem for me when around people; he is courteous and mannerly with me. _____

16. He avoids being a nitpicker, making mountains out of molehills. _____

17. He loves sharing his ideas, interests, and life with me. _____

18. He listens to me even when I am telling him something in which he is not particularly interested. _____

19. He is a fun person to be with; he takes life and himself seriously, but not too seriously. _____

20. He tries to change any habits that are annoying to me. _____

21. He tries to see things from my perspective and is interested in my viewpoints. _____

22. He tries to love me in the way I want to be loved. _____

23. He exercises spiritual leadership, setting an example of servanthood, leading in devotions, praying regularly for and with me. _____

24. He is sensitive to my problems and difficulties and tries to be an encouragement to me. _____

25. He acts like I am the most important person in his life next to the Lord; he treats me like I am really valuable; he communicates appreciation. _____

List items on which you would like to see improvement.

10

Being a Wife

𝒢 od has a plan for husband/wife relationships. It's a good plan because He is a good, merciful and all-wise God. Understanding and following His plan is the pathway to marital bliss and a part of real wisdom. Ignoring or distorting His plan is foolish and disastrous.

In session 9, you learned God's plan for husbands in marriage. Ideally, you were able to come to an agreement on what a husband should be in God's kind of marriage. Similarly, this session on God's plan for wives will help you explore the same mindedness on this important aspect of marriage.

So roll up your sleeves, pray fervently for God's assistance, put on your thinking cap, pick up Bible and pen, find a quiet place, and go to work on the following assignments.

Assignments:

1. *The Ideal Wife.* Each one of you writes a brief article built on the phrases: "An ideal wife is..." and "In marriage, I think the wife should..." In the article, be specific, practical, clear, concrete, and as thorough as possible. Study Genesis 2:18–25; Proverbs 18:22; 31:10–31; Ephesians 5:22–33; Titus 2:4–5; and 1 Peter 3:1–8 as you write this article. Now share your "ideal wife" assignments with each other. Compare what each of you wrote, and discuss all similarities and differences. What would you add, subtract, change, expand, or correct to make what you wrote more biblical and useful?

2. *Scorecard for Future Wives.* Note that there is one form for the wife-to-be and another for the husband-to-be. Discuss your evaluations with each other.

3. *Interview.* Get together with a godly, successful wife and interview her on what it means to be God's kind of wife. Ask her questions such as: What are the wife's God-given responsibilities to her husband? What does the Bible mean by submission? What does it involve? What does it mean for the wife to be her husband's helper? How can a wife be in submission and yet not stifle or neglect her God-given abilities? How can a wife remind, correct, and advise her husband without being bossy or nagging? What are the most important factors in being a godly wife?

SCORECARD FOR FUTURE WIVES (HERS)

Use this inventory to evaluate yourself as a potential wife. This inventory enumerates issues that are important factors in a good husband/wife relationship. If you are going to be the kind of wife God wants you to be, the factors that will make you that kind of wife will be evident in your life right now. On those statements where you score high (4 or 3), praise God and make sure you keep on doing these things. On those items where your score is 2 or lower, accept the challenge and work on improving.

RATING SCALE:
4 = Regularly
3 = Frequently
2 = Sometimes
1 = Rarely
0 = Never

1. I take pride in my bedroom, apartment, or home by making it attractive and cheerful. _____

2. I handle my finances responsibly. _____

3. I keep myself attractive in appearance so that my partner is glad to have everyone know that I am the woman he plans to marry. _____

4. I am a good sport, cheerful, uncomplaining, appreciative, and not a nag. _____

5. I am willing to let my partner have his own way and the last word when we disagree. _____

6. I avoid making a fuss over minor problems that I should handle alone. _____

7. I show respect and admiration for my partner, not comparing him unfavorably with other men, but making him know that I esteem him above all other men. _____

8. I show courtesy and consideration to his parents and to his other relatives. _____

9. I take a sympathetic and intelligent interest in his work, yet leave him a free hand, realizing that he must sometimes give time to his work that we would rather have together. _____

10. I cultivate an interest in his friends and recreations so that I can make a satisfactory partner of his leisure hours. _____

11. I pray regularly with and for my partner and maintain a good devotional life. _____

12. I seek his counsel on important decisions. _____

13. I support his decisions and cheerfully assist him in fulfilling them. _____

14. I show respect and esteem for him around other people. _____

15. I lovingly share my ideas, problems, joys, interests, and affection with him on a regular basis. _____

16. I avoid shouting and screaming at him. _____

17. I refrain from using force or threats or punishment to get my own way. _____

18. I avoid allowing my friends or activities to interfere with time to fulfill his desires. _____

19. I refrain from embarrassing him or putting him down. _____

20. I keep myself internally as well as externally attractive. _____

21. I am a fun person to be with. _____

22. I keep appointments, am on time for dates, call if my plans are changed. _____

23. I accept responsibilities and faithfully fulfill them. _____

24. I am sensitive to his problems and difficulties and try to be an encouragement to him. _____

25. I try to change habits that are annoying to him. _____

Go back over these questions and note every question you rated 2 or below. The content of these questions will give you ideas on how you can improve. Also, note the questions you answered with a 3 or 4. These are areas where you are doing fine. Keep them in mind so you will continue to do them.

SCORECARD FOR FUTURE WIVES (HIS)

Use this inventory to evaluate your future wife.

RATING SCALE:
4 = Regularly
3 = Frequently
2 = Sometimes
1 = Rarely
0 = Never

1. She tries to make her apartment or home interesting, attractive, and cheerful, devoting as much thought and study to it as she would to a job downtown. _____

2. She handles the finances that are her responsibility in a businesslike fashion. _____

3. She keeps herself attractive (though not offensively so) so that I am glad to have everyone know that she is to be my wife. _____

4. She is a good sport, cheerful, uncomplaining, appreciative, and not a nag. _____

5. She is willing to let me have my own way and the last word when we disagree. _____

6. She avoids making a fuss over trifles and solves minor problems that she should handle alone. _____

7. She shows respect and admiration for me, not comparing me unfavorably with other men, but making me think that she esteems me above all other men. _____

8. She prevents her mother and other relatives from intruding unduly, and shows courtesy and consideration to my relatives. _____

9. She takes a sympathetic and intelligent interest in my work, yet leaves me a free hand, realizing that I must sometimes give time to my work that I would rather have with her. _____

10. She cultivates an interest in my friends and recreation, so that she can make a satisfactory partner of my leisure hours.   _____

11. She prays regularly with and for me and maintains a good devotional life.   _____

12. She seeks my counsel on important decisions.   _____

13. She supports my decisions and cheerfully assists me in fulfilling them.   _____

14. She shows respect and esteem for me around other people.   _____

15. She lovingly shares her ideas, problems, joys, interests, and affection on a regular basis.   _____

16. She avoids shouting and screaming at me.   _____

17. She refrains from using force or threats or punishing me to get her own way.   _____

18. She avoids allowing her friends or activities to interfere with time to fulfill my desires.   _____

19. She refrains from embarrassing me or putting me down.   _____

20. She keeps herself internally as well as externally attractive.   _____

21. She is a fun person to be with.   _____

22. She keeps appointments, is on time for dates, and calls if plans are changed.   _____

23. She accepts responsibilities and faithfully fulfills them.   _____

24. She is sensitive to my problems and tries to be an encouragement to me.   _____

25. She tries to change any habits that are annoying to me.   _____

List items on which you would like to see improvement.

11

Family Finances

"Money isn't everything in life, but it's far ahead of whatever else is in second place." This quip made by who knows who was probably spoken in jest. Unfortunately, it does depict the attitude that many have toward money.

Instinctively we know that there is something wrong with this attitude. Yet all too often many of us act as if it were true. We behave as if money were the most important thing in life, as if our very lives consisted in the abundance of things that we possess. We make decisions based primarily upon the financial rewards we will receive. We think of it, dream of it, work for it, hoard it, waste it, count it, and recount it. It becomes a dominant, perhaps *the* dominant, theme of our lives.

Others (probably fewer in number) react against this love of money with a disdain for money. They guard against materialism. They believe in the simple lifestyle. They may even make decisions based on their disdain for money. Their motto may be: if it is financially rewarding or costly, it probably is wrong. They may avoid certain things and refuse to purchase certain things or go to certain places because of the money involved.

Indeed, there are differing opinions about money, and these conflicting views can have a devastating effect on people and relationships. Conflicting ideas about finances are often a part of marital dysfunction. In fact, in some cases the major complaint against the other person involves money.

This fact raises a very important question for Christians contemplating marriage: What is God's plan for family finances? What should a

Christian's attitude toward money be? How does God want you to handle your finances?

In His Word, God has given clear, solid guidelines and principles for viewing and handling finances. In this session, you will be directed into a practical and highly beneficial study of these principles.

So roll up your sleeves, pray fervently for God's help, find a quiet place, pick up Bible and pen, put on your thinking cap, and go to work on the following assignments. Allow God to use His Word to challenge and mold your thoughts in this very important area of your life and relationship. As you explore this subject, let God bring the two of you to same mindedness.

Assignments:

1. *Handling Family Finances*

2. *Personal Financial Profile*

3. *First-Year Budget.* God has called us to be good stewards of all that He has given us. This includes our money. To be a good steward, it is important that we plan and budget to do so.

4. *Discussion with others.* God has not left us alone in this world to fend for ourselves. He has given us His Word and His Spirit to lead and guide us. He has also given us other believers to help us grow more like Jesus. Use this resource that God has given you by discussing with a godly couple some or all of the questions included in this book. Ask them about financial issues or conflicts that have arisen in their relationship and how they have resolved or are attempting to resolve them. Pick their brains and learn all you can from them that will help you to handle your family finances God's way.

5. *Counting differences.* If living at home, determine what each of you are costing your parents. Also determine the income and expenditures of each of your families and identify the possible effects of any differences. If you are not living at home and are supporting yourselves, each of you should fulfill the same assignment with this alteration in mind.

6. *Planning ahead.* Estimate when the greatest periods of financial needs will probably occur and plan how you will prepare for them.

7. *Your response.* Write a brief summary of your response to these assignments; note how they challenged and helped you, as well as potential problem areas and questions that you would like to ask.

HANDLING FAMILY FINANCES

Discuss and record your personal views about:

1. The basis on which you will select your occupation and place of employment

2. Credit buying, charge accounts, and loans

3. Savings accounts and investments

4. Giving to the church, needy people, parents, and children

5. Spending money on amusements, entertainment, recreation, and vacation

6. Financial planning, budgeting, and bookkeeping

7. The husband working overtime or having a second job

8. Having a job that requires you to work evenings and be away from home for periods of time

9. The wife taking a job

10. Financial priorities (furniture or automobile, husband's or wife's clothing, etc.)

11. Insurance

12. Making out a will

13. Providing for emergencies

14. Who will pay the bills and handle routine financial affairs

15. Buying or spending without the other person's agreement

16. Providing for old age

17. Going out to dinner

18. Buying or renting a home

19. Joint or separate bank accounts

20. Spending money on gifts for each other

21. How much should be spent on clothes, furniture, automobiles, hobbies, etc.

Discuss and record the attitudes your respective parents had toward money. Were they savers or spenders? Were they conscientious about paying bills? Did they budget their money? Did they spend money for luxuries or only for necessities? Were they generous in giving to the church and others? Was making money a major focus of their lives? Did they make joint decisions about money? Did your mother have money apportioned to her for spending? Who was in charge of the finances? Did they keep good records? Did your mother work? Did they have joint or separate bank accounts? Did they have a savings account, insurance, or investments? Did they buy new automobiles or furniture frequently? Did they frequently repaint or redecorate? Were they self-producers? (Evaluate how your respective parents differed and where your attitudes and financial outlook is like theirs and different from your spouse's. Your differing viewpoints may be fertile soil for bitterness, irritation, and resentment unless you can come to a mutually satisfying agreement. Discuss how you can resolve your differences.)

List a number of truths about finances found in:

1. 1 Chronicles 29:11–12

2. Psalm 24:1

3. Proverbs 3:9–10

4. Proverbs 6:6–8

5. Proverbs 10:4; 11:24–25, 28; 12:10; 13:11, 24; 15:16–17, 22; 16:8, 16

6. Proverbs 16:3; 21:5

7. Proverbs 19:22; 20:18; 27:23–24

8. Luke 14:28

9. Romans 13:6–8

10. Ephesians 4:28

11. 1 Thessalonians 4:10–12

12. 1 Timothy 6:3–10, 17–18

PERSONAL FINANCIAL PROFILE

Estimate the value for each item below you own:

Item	Estimated Value
Home (owned since _____)	$_____
Car (number owned _____)	$_____
Furnishings	$_____
Savings	$_____
Investments	$_____
Loans due you	$_____
Collections (stamps, coins)	$_____
Life insurance (cash surrender value)	$_____
Other assets	$_____

List what you currently owe:

Item	Total	Monthly Payment
Home mortgage(s)	$_____	$_____
Car loan(s)	$_____	$_____
Personal loan(s)	$_____	$_____
Credit card(s)	$_____	$_____
Store loan(s)	$_____	$_____
Other debts		
_____	$_____	$_____
_____	$_____	$_____
_____	$_____	$_____

FIRST-YEAR BUDGET

Try to complete this form as realistically as possible. Make an educated guess about the items where you don't know the exact cost.

FLEXIBLE EXPENSES

Furniture/household equipment/repairs	$_____
Medical and dental care	$_____
Vacation and travel (include honeymoon if not paid before wedding)	$_____
Christmas, birthdays, and other gifts	$_____
Education/schooling	$_____
Entertainment/hobbies/recreation	$_____
Allowances/lunches	$_____
Occupational/business expenses	$_____

Living Expenses

Food and household supplies	$_____
Cleaning and laundry	$_____
Personal supplies (cosmetics, haircuts, clothes, etc.)	$_____
Newspapers, magazines, books, subscriptions	$_____

Transportation

Automobile purchases and/or monthly payments	$_____
Automobile operation/maintenance (gas, oil, repairs)	$_____
Total Flexible Expenses	$_____

FIXED EXPENSES

Tithes and offerings to the church	$_____
Charitable contributions other than to the church	$_____
Housing (rent or mortgage)	$_____
Vehicle licenses and driver's licenses	$_____
Professional or union dues	$_____
Organizational memberships	$_____
Professional journals	$_____

Taxes

Property $_____

School $_____

Other assessments $_____

Federal income tax $_____

State/local taxes $_____

Utilities

Heat (gas, oil) $_____

Electric $_____

Telephone $_____

Water $_____

Sewer/garbage $_____

Insurance

Automobile $_____

Life $_____

Hospitalization/health/medical $_____

Homeowners/apartment dwellers $_____

Other _____ $_____

Installment Payments

Loans (other than automobile or mortgage) $_____

Department stores $_____

Credit cards $_____

Savings/investments $_____

Other debt $_____

Total Fixed Expenses $_____

SUMMARY/TABULATION

Total flexible expenses	$_____
+ Total fixed expenses	$_____
= Total Expenses	$_____
Income of husband (take home)	$_____
+ Income of wife (take home)	$_____
= Total Income	$_____
Total income	$_____
– Total expenses	$_____
Difference + or –	$_____

If your expenses are greater than your income, check your arithmetic to be sure you added correctly. Also, check each item to confirm that you estimated expenses realistically. If your expenses are greater than your income, discuss how and where you can decrease expenses or increase income.

12

Sex as God Intended

Sex is one of the great gifts God has given to men and women. Within the confines of the marriage relationship, it is intended to be a beautiful expression of unity and oneness. Unfortunately, as you are certainly aware, mankind has perverted this wonderful gift and destroyed the beauty of God's plan.

In my marriage counseling, I have become increasingly aware of the heartache that people encounter because of problems in their sexual relationship. Complaints about sexual disagreements and disappointments seem to be a common factor with many couples, whether they are Christian or not.

On the one hand, some people see sex relations as the fulcrum of the entire relationship, the most important thing in life. If the bells don't ring and the bands don't constantly play, their marriage and their lives are total disasters. How things are going in their sexual relationship becomes the measuring stick by which everything is evaluated.

On the other hand, there are individuals who consider sexual relations unpleasant and distasteful. Or they see sexual relations as unimportant and unnecessary. Sex may be necessary if you want to have children, but beyond that it has no purpose, they believe.

Occasionally, these individuals may be willing to pacify their partners who have a much stronger sexual interest. Personally, however, they would be willing to forego this aspect of marriage almost entirely. Either they have no desire for sex or they have an intense aversion to it.

This scenario is only one of many that occur in marital conflict over sex relations. The actual particulars of what is involved in sexual conflict may vary. The point is that whatever those particulars may be, they can be the context in which great marital distress and misery is experienced.

Indeed, exploring this aspect of the marital relationship carefully is no small matter. It's a vital part of preparing for marriage God's way.

As you focus on this subject, be open and honest about the items you are going to discuss. If you feel a little embarrassed talking about sexual things with each other or your counselor or teacher, don't back off; ask God for help and press on.

In His Word, God has given much information and many directions about sex relations. And when He does, He doesn't stutter or blush or hide His face. True, He says it discreetly and in a wholesome way. But *he says it*.

Reflect on the fact that if God's Word openly speaks about sex, then it must be all right, even important, for you to reflect on it. It follows also that it must be appropriate (even necessary) for your godly counselor or teacher to openly yet discreetly discuss a biblical perspective on sex relations with you.

Please be open and honest with your counselor or teacher about your feelings and thoughts. If you feel embarrassed or think that the issues considered are too personal, share that with your counselor, along with your feelings and thoughts.

So roll up your sleeves, pray for God's help, find a quiet place, pick up Bible and pen, put on your thinking cap, and go to work on the following assignments.

Assignments:

1. *The Marriage Act*

2. *Questions for Sexual Discussion*

3. *Your response.* Write a brief summary of your response to these assignments, how they challenged you and helped you, potential problem areas, and any questions you would like to ask.

4. *License requirements.* If it is appropriate (depending upon the date of your wedding and the laws of your particular state), schedule an appointment to see your physician for a complete physical examination, for birth control information, if desired, and for a blood test. You will need to have a physical examination and blood test to apply for your marriage license.

THE MARRIAGE ACT

1. Study Genesis 1:27–28; 2:18–25; Proverbs 5:15–19; 1 Corinthians
   7:2–5; and Ephesians 5:22–33 and determine several purposes
   of marriage.

2. Write your own paraphrase of Hebrews 13:4 (you may want to
   compare a number of translations before you do).

3. List a number of truths about sexual relations found in Proverbs 5:15–21; Song of Solomon 4:1–7; 5:10–16; 7:1–10; and 1 Corinthians 7:2–5.

4. Study Acts 20:35 and Philippians 2:3–4 and determine how the principles of these verses can be applied to sexual relations.

5. If birth control is a problem for you, study the following verses and see if anything in them is of help in this regard: Genesis 1:27–28; Exodus 20:13; Proverbs 5:15–20; 14:15; 22:3; 1 Corinthians 7:2–5; Ephesians 5:25, 28–29; Philippians 2:4; 1 Timothy 5:8; and James 2:17–20.

6. As God looked upon Adam and Eve having sexual relations, what do you think was His attitude? What is your attitude as you anticipate sexual relations in marriage? Do you have any fears? What place should sex relations have in a marriage relationship? How often should a couple have sex relations? What should a couple do if they have problems in this area of their marriage?

7. Are the following statements true or false?

   a. Married people should freely tell each other what pleases them in sex relations.   T   F

   b. At times it's all right to make excuses to avoid sexual relationships.   T   F

   c. Using street language or harsh language is a good practice in reference to sex relations.   T   F

   d. Men can enjoy sex more than women.   T   F

   e. Strong sexual desire in marriage is a sign of a lack of spirituality.   T   F

   f. Married people should freely discuss their sexual relationship with each other.   T   F

   g. Married people should be free to tell each other that sex is not appealing to them occasionally.   T   F

   h. Since a couple's sexual relationship is a private matter, if problems occur they should not seek help from someone outside the marriage.   T   F

   i. Women should not initiate sex relations.   T   F

   j. In many cases the biggest hindrance to good sexual relations is a negative attitude.   T   F

   k. Whatever is mutually enjoyable and fulfilling to the couple and does not hurt anyone or violate biblical principles is proper in the confines of a couple's bedroom.   T   F

   l. God is pleased when a married couple has sex.   T   F

   m. God intended sex to be fun, satisfying, and desirable for the husband and wife.   T   F

   n. Sexual bargaining is wrong.   T   F

   o. Selfishness in sexual relations is forbidden by Scripture.   T   F

   p. Selfishness may be manifested in withholding sex or in demanding sex.   T   F

q. Sex relations in marriage are to be regular and continuous.　　　　　T　　F

r. Abstinence from sexual relationships in marriage is a sign of deep spirituality.　　　　　T　　F

s. In marriage, every sexual urge should be followed.　　　　　T　　F

t. Frequency of sex relations should be regulated by the satisfaction principle.　　　　　T　　F

u. A person shouldn't think about having sex with his or her spouse.　　　　　T　　F

v. Intercourse equals sex relations.　　　　　T　　F

w. Sexual problems (hang-ups) are often symptoms of personal problems or relationship problems.　　　　　T　　F

QUESTIONS FOR SEXUAL DISCUSSION

Write your answers to the following questions individually. Then discuss them with each other. Bring your answers and any additional questions or concerns about sex to the next session, for discussion with your counselor or teacher.

1. Do you recall any specific event or events that have influenced your attitude toward, feelings, and thoughts about sex? Explain.

2. What was your parents' attitude toward sex?

3. What did you learn from your parents about sex directly or indirectly, verbally or nonverbally?

4. Did your parents talk freely to you about sex? What did they say? What kind of instruction did they give you?

5. Did you talk to your parents about your sexual concerns? Did you ask them questions? If so, what kind of questions? Did they answer these questions with or without embarrassment? Were you satisfied with the answers they gave?

6. Was physical affection shown freely by your parents to one another and to you and your brothers and sisters?

7. Do you recall playing sex games as a child? If so, how did you feel as you were involved in playing these games? Were you discovered playing these games? What happened? What was your reaction to what happened?

8. What stirs up sexual guilt or shame in you now? What embarrasses you about sex?

9. When did you learn where babies come from and how they are conceived? How did you learn? How did you react to this information?

10. As you anticipate marriage, what are your thoughts about sexual intercourse? What are your expectations? What causes some concern or apprehension?

11. Describe your concept of the differences between men and women in the area of sex. Is there any difference? If so, what is it? What roles or activities should the husband perform in sex relations? What roles or activities should the wife perform?

12. What form(s) of contraceptives will you use? Do you and your partner agree? Do you fully understand how the contraceptives you have chosen work? Are you aware of any side effects? How reliable are they?

13. Have you and your partner talked about children? Have you agreed on the number of children you would like to have? When would you like to start a family? Have you agreed on when you want to begin having children? Have you discussed how far apart (time wise) you want to attempt to space your children?

13

Your Special Day

*C*ongratulations! By this time, you have completed twelve sessions designed to prepare you for your upcoming marriage. You've been giving serious attention to preparing for marriage God's way. Surely you've expended effort and have benefited from this endeavor.

Now you have a deeper and broader understanding of God's desires for your marriage. Already you're beginning to reap the results of your faithful efforts. Already you've been able to apply what you have considered in your life and relationship.

As a result of these studies, one of two things should have occurred. You are either more ready for marriage, or you've come to the conclusion that you are not ready for marriage, at least not right now.

Either way, your efforts have been beneficial. If you've decided that you shouldn't get married right away, your decision has been a painful one. If you're not prepared for marriage God's way, you will be preventing something from occurring that may be even more painful and disastrous. In the long run, that will be beneficial.

Make sure that your concerns and reasons for postponement are justified. Be aware that most people experience some fears and hesitation as the wedding day approaches. It's quite normal to experience some ambivalence! After all, marriage is a serious business. For Christians, it's until death do you part. The privileges and responsibilities are many, and many changes will take place.

Don't make more out of your fears than you legitimately should. At the same time, if you have good reasons for thinking you are not ready to build your marriage God's way, don't ignore those convictions. As a counselor who has seen the devastation caused when unprepared people get married, I commend you for the maturity and honesty to acknowledge it. I also urge you to seek personal help concerning the reasons for your decision.

Most who complete this course have had a different experience. For you, working through *Preparing for Marriage God's Way* has increased your desire and readiness for marriage. Now you're more eager to marry than you were when you began. You see real growth in yourself, your partner, and your relationship. You're longing for the time when the two of you will become one as you are joined together in holy wedlock.

If that's the case, let's proceed with the four main purposes for this session.

Review

Consolidate and assess what you have accomplished during the last twelve sessions. To facilitate this goal, review the material covered in every previous session. Write down the most important principles from every session. Evaluate how you are doing in applying these principles. Be ready to share examples of how you are succeeding or failing.

Loose Ends

Think through and write down issues that you would like to consider in this session. They may be issues that were not discussed to your satisfaction or ones that were not even explored.

Wedding Plans

In this session, you will be finalizing wedding details. Keep in mind that your wedding ceremony is a worship service. It is a worship service in which God's people assemble to thank Him for the gift of marriage and to witness a solemn giving and receiving of vows. It is also a worship service in which the two of you will thank God for each other and covenant yourselves to each other before God for as long as you both shall live. Keep this truth in mind as you plan your special day.

As you prepare for this big day, don't allow the many last-minute wedding details to rob you of the joy and excitement that this day should hold. Remember, the most important thing about the day is not how the flowers look or the color of the bridesmaids' dresses. The most important thing about your wedding day is that you will come as two and leave as one. *Rejoice* and be exceedingly glad, for God has been good to you!

Be sure to spend time individually and unitedly thinking about what kind of ceremony you want to have. What special music are you going to have? Are you going to write your own vows or do you want to choose prewritten vows? What topic would you like the pastor to focus on during his meditation?

Your Honeymoon

The fourth purpose of this session is preparation for a good, beneficial honeymoon. Probably by now you have planned a lot of the details of your honeymoon. Enjoy the thrill of arranging your first vacation as husband and wife!

In many ways, your honeymoon can be the best vacation of your life. However, for some who are not adequately prepared, it is a very hard experience. Don't let that happen to you. Let your honeymoon be a pleasant experience that you will remember with joy. Plan your honeymoon prayerfully, intelligently, carefully, and unitedly. Discuss your honeymoon with your counselor or teacher.

On your honeymoon, don't allow yourself to become so worked up that you forget all that you have learned during these thirteen training sessions. Reflect on what you have studied. Rely on the Lord, step out in faith and deal in love with any problems that may arise. Love does cover a multitude of sins (1 Peter 4:8). And, if you really get stuck, call your counselor or teacher. Yes, even while you are on your honeymoon! *Do not let any little problems remain unsolved!* Remember, it only takes a little match to start a giant fire.

PART TWO

AFTER THE WEDDING

(14)

Six-Week Checkup

Assignments:

1. On the day before this session, fill out *Rate Your Marriage*. Circle the numbers representing items that cause you any concern.

2. Make a journal of the high points and low points of your relationship from the wedding until this session. Note any conflicts, problems, and annoyances that have arisen and how you handled or resolved them.

3. Keep a family devotional, a spiritual life journal. Note what you have studied together, how your corporate prayer life is going, difficulties you have faced in this area, how you have helped and are helping one another to grow spiritually, as well as any questions or concerns you may have.

4. Write down any issues or questions you want to discuss with your counselor or teacher and bring them with you to the next session.

RATE YOUR MARRIAGE

This inventory is designed to evaluate how you are doing in your marriage relationship and to identify problem areas so that you may work on correcting them. The inventory will be most beneficial if you take it individually and then sit down and discuss your respective answers to each question. Seek to understand clearly your spouse's reasons for giving the rating that he or she did. If your ratings pinpoint some difficulties, focus on how to resolve problems. Don't just attack or blame your spouse. It will be of no benefit for you to defend yourself. Remember, God does have a solution to every problem if you will only handle your problems and seek to solve them in a biblical way. View and use this inventory in a constructive way.

RATING SCALE:
4 = Always
3 = Often/frequently
2 = Sometimes
1 = Seldom
0 = Never

Write the number that describes what you judge to be true of your marriage in the blank following each question.

1. Does the fact that Jesus Christ is Lord manifest itself in practical ways in your marriage? _____

2. Do you use the Bible to determine your convictions, decisions, and practices in life in general and marriage in particular? _____

3. Do you and your spouse study the Bible and pray together? _____

4. Do you worship God together with other believers? _____

5. Do you serve God together in activities that will build up the church and honor Christ? _____

6. Do you and your spouse seek to please one another? _____

7. Do you ask for forgiveness when you have done something wrong?   _____

8. Do you take full responsibility for your thoughts, actions, and reactions?   _____

9. Do you allow your spouse to disagree with you without becoming nasty or punishing him or her?   _____

10. Do you allow your spouse to make mistakes without becoming nasty or punishing him or her?   _____

11. Do you focus on the things that are commendable, praiseworthy, and good about your spouse?   _____

12. Do you express appreciation to your spouse in tangible ways? Do you express gratitude and thanks?   _____

13. Do you communicate in an in-depth way with each other daily?   _____

14. Do you express your opinions, ideas, plans, aspirations, fears, feelings, likes, dislikes, views, problems, joys, frustrations, and annoyances to each other?   _____

15. Do you and your spouse understand each other when you try to express yourselves?   _____

16. Do you do many different things together and enjoy being with each other? Are you involved in common projects?   _____

17. Do you show love in many practical and tangible ways?   _____

18. Do you still court one another by occasional gifts, unexpected attention, etc.?   _____

19. Is your conversation pleasant and friendly?   _____

20. Do you pray for one another, support, and seek to encourage one another?   _____

21. Can you discuss differing viewpoints on values, priorities, religious convictions, politics, etc., without becoming irritated?   _____

22. Do you anticipate sexual relations with your spouse? _____

23. Are your sexual desires compatible? _____

24. Do you freely discuss your sexual desires with your spouse? _____

25. Do you agree about the way money should be spent? _____

26. Do you think your spouse is as concerned about your views on the way money should be spent as he or she is about his or her own? _____

27. Do you agree on how to bring up children? _____

28. Do you refuse to lie to your spouse; are you building your relationship on speaking the truth? Can your spouse put full confidence in whatever you say, knowing that you really mean what you say? _____

29. Do you have a good relationship with your in-laws? Do you appreciate them? _____

30. Do you really respect your spouse? _____

31. Are you glad to introduce your spouse to friends and associates? _____

32. Do you control yourself when you are moody so that you do not disrupt your relationship and inflict your moodiness on others? _____

33. Do you seek to change your specific habits that may cause discomfort or displeasure to your spouse? _____

34. Do you make your relationship with your spouse a priority matter? _____

35. Do you treat your spouse with respect and dignity? _____

36. Do you accept corrective criticisms graciously? _____

37. Do you agree concerning the roles and responsibilities of husband and wife? _____

38. Are you willing to face, discuss, and look for scriptural solutions to problems without blowing up or attacking your spouse or dissolving into tears? _____

39. Do you maintain your own spiritual life through Bible reading, prayer, regular church attendance, and fellowship with God's people? _____

Total: _____

Put a circle around the number of any of the previous items that give you any concern about your relationship.

15

Six-Month Checkup

Assignments:

1. Do the *Ways a Husband Loves His Wife* and *Ways a Wife Loves Her Husband* studies.

2. Choose a two-week period in which you will keep a good times/bad times journal.

3. Carefully read and discuss the items on *Parenting Commitments*. Identify for learning, not condemning purposes, how you perceive your family of origin functioned on each of these items. Discuss the possible impact on your own parenting.

4. A day or two before this session, fill out *Rate Your Marriage*. Follow the same procedure for *Communication Test 1* and *2*.

5. Write down any issues or questions you want to discuss with your counselor or teacher and bring them with you to the next session.

WAYS A HUSBAND LOVES HIS WIFE

The following list sets forth practical ways a husband may express his love to his wife. Use it as a guide to help you evaluate the way you express love to your wife. Circle any ideas you are neglecting that show your wife you love her. Ask her to go over the list and put a check mark in front of the ways she would like you to express love, and to add other things to the list.

You may express love to your wife by:

1. Functioning as the loving leader of your home.

2. Telling her frequently that you love her.

3. Giving her a regular amount of money to spend in any way she chooses.

4. Leading family devotions regularly.

5. Smiling and being cheerful when you come home from work.

6. Helping her wash and dry the dishes or doing them yourself so that she might have time for herself to relax (at least twice a week).

7. Taking her out to dinner or to do some fun thing at least once a week.

8. Doing "fix-it" jobs she wants done around the house (when she wants them done).

9. Greeting her when you come home with a smile, a hug, a kiss, and an "Am I glad to see you. I really missed you today." (If she works and comes home after you, then greet her in the same way when she returns home.)

10. Giving her a lingering kiss.

11. Patting her on the shoulder or some other region of her anatomy; holding her hand or caressing her frequently.

12. Being willing to talk to her about her concerns and not belittling her for having those concerns.

13. Looking at her with an adoring expression.

14. Sitting close to her.

15. Rubbing her back or . . .

16. Shaving or taking a shower or brushing your teeth before you have sex relations.

17. Wearing her favorite aftershave lotion.

18. Writing love notes or letters to her.

19. Letting her know that you appreciate her and what you appreciate about her. Do this often and for things that are sometimes taken for granted. Pretend you are trying to convince her you think she is great and very important to you.

20. Fulfilling her implied or unspoken desires or wishes, as well as the specific requests she makes of you. Anticipate what she might desire and surprise her by doing it before she asks.

21. Playing with her; sharing her hobbies and recreational preferences enthusiastically; including her in yours.

22. Seeking to set a good example.

23. Talking about her favorably to others when she can hear you and when she cannot.

24. Bragging about her good points as a wife and in every other area to others; letting her know that you are proud to have her as your wife.

25. Maintaining your own spiritual life through Bible study, prayer, regular church attendance, and fellowship with God's people.

26. Handling your affairs decently and in order; structuring your time and using it wisely.

27. Making plans prayerfully and carefully.

28. Asking her advice when you have problems or decisions to make.

29. Following her advice unless doing so would violate biblical principles.

30. Fulfilling your responsibilities.

31. Being sober, but not somber, about life.

32. Having a realistic, biblical, positive attitude toward life.

33. Discussing plans with your wife before you make decisions, and when the plans are made, sharing them fully with her, giving reasons for making the decisions you did.

34. Thanking her in creative ways for her attempts to please you.

35. Actually changing where and when you should.

36. Sharing your insights, reading, and good experiences with her.

37. Planning for a mini-honeymoon where the two of you can do whatever you want to do.

38. Giving a low whistle or some other expression of admiration when she wears a new dress or your favorite negligee or . . .

39. Gently brushing her leg under the table.

40. Being reasonably happy to go shopping with her.

41. Relating what happened at work or whatever you did apart from her.

42. Reminiscing about the early days of your courtship.

43. Expressing appreciation for her parents and relatives.

44. Taking her out to breakfast.

45. Agreeing with her about getting a new dress or some other item.

46. Thanking her when she supports your decisions and cooperates enthusiastically. Especially make it a matter of celebration when she supports and helps enthusiastically at times when you know that she doesn't fully agree.

47. Asking her to have sexual relations with you and seeking to be especially solicitous of her desires. Express gratitude when she tries to please you.

48. Buying gifts for her.

49. Watching her television programs or going where she wants to go instead of watching or doing what you want. Do it cheerfully and enthusiastically.

50. Being cooperative and appreciative when she holds, caresses, or kisses you.

51. Running errands gladly.

52. Pampering her and making a fuss over her.

53. Being willing to see things from her point of view.

54. Being lovingly honest with her—no backdoor messages or withholding of the truth that may hinder your present or future relationship.

55. Indicating you want to be alone with her to talk or just lie in each other's arms.

56. Refusing to cop out, blow up, attack, blame shift, withdraw, or exaggerate when she seeks to make constructive suggestions or discuss problems.

57. Giving her your undivided attention when she wants to talk.

58. Cheerfully staying up until ____ o'clock to solve a problem or share her burdens.

59. Holding her close while expressing tangible and vocal love when she is hurt, discouraged, weary, or burdened.

60. Planning vacations and trips with her.

61. Being eager to share a good joke or some other interesting information you have learned.

62. Going with her in a team ministry in the church.

63. Going to a Bible study or research project together.

64. Establishing and following a family budget.

65. Keeping yourself attractive and neat.

66. Being cooperative and helpful, and functioning as a cohost when you have people in for dinner or fellowship.

67. Asking her to pray with you about something.

68. Acknowledging that there are some specific areas or ways in which you need to improve.

69. Refusing to disagree with her in the presence of others.

70. Cooperating with her in establishing family goals and then in fulfilling them.

71. Being available and eager to fulfill her desires whenever and wherever possible and proper.

72. Beginning each day with cheerfulness and tangible expressions of affection.

73. Planning to spend some time alone with her each day for sharing and communicating.

74. Remembering to tell her when you must work late.

75. Refusing to work late on a regular basis.

76. Taking care of the yard work properly.

77. Refusing to compare her unfavorably with other people.

78. Handling money wisely.

79. Not allowing work, church, or recreational activities to keep you from fulfilling marriage responsibilities.

80. Trying to find things to do with her.

81. Being willing to go out or stay home with her.

82. Being polite and courteous and mannerly with her.

83. Refusing to be overly dependent on your parents or friends.

84. Developing mutual friends.

85. Providing hospitalization insurance.

86. Trying to the level of your ability to provide housing and some support for your family in case you should die or become handicapped.

WAYS A WIFE LOVES HER HUSBAND

The following list sets forth practical ways a wife may express her love to her husband. Use it as a guide to help you evaluate the way you express love to your husband. Circle any ideas you are neglecting which show your husband you love him. Ask him to go over the list and put a check mark in front of the ways he would like you to express love, and to add other things to the list.

You may express love to your husband by:

1. Greeting him at the door when he comes home with a smile, a hug, a kiss and an "Am I glad to see you. I really missed you today."

2. Having a cup of coffee or tea (or his favorite beverage) ready for him when he comes home from work.

3. Giving him a lingering kiss.

4. Letting him know you like to be with him and making arrangements so you can spend time with him without giving the impression that you really should or would rather be doing something else.

5. Being willing to talk with him about his concerns and not belittling him for having those concerns.

6. Supporting him and cooperating with him enthusiastically and positively when he has made a decision.

7. Teasing him and flirting with him.

8. Seeking to arouse him and sometimes being the aggressor or leader in sex relations.

9. Asking him to have sex relations more than he would expect you to.

10. Letting yourself go when having sexual relations.

11. Caressing him.

12. Looking at him with an adoring expression.

13. Holding his hand.

14. Sitting close to him.

15. Rubbing his back or . . .

16. Wearing his favorite nightgown or dress or perfume or . . .

17. Expressing your love in words or notes.

18. Letting him know that you appreciate him and what you appreciate about him. Do this often and for things that are sometimes taken for granted. Pretend you are trying to convince him you think he is great and very important to you.

19. Standing with him and supporting him in his attempt to live for God.

20. Fulfilling his implied or unspoken desires or wishes, as well as the specific requests he makes of you. Anticipate what he might desire and surprise him by doing it before he asks.

21. Playing with him (tennis, golf, party games, etc.); sharing his hobbies and recreational preferences enthusiastically; including him in yours.

22. Enthusiastically cooperating with him and sharing with him in devotions and prayer.

23. Maintaining your own spiritual life through Bible study, prayer, regular church attendance, and fellowship with God's people.

24. Handling your affairs decently and in order; structuring your time and using it wisely.

25. Being willing to face and solve problems even if it requires discomfort, change, and much effort.

26. Fulfilling your responsibilities.

27. Asking his advice when you have problems or decisions to make.

28. Following his advice unless doing so would violate biblical principles.

29. Being ready to leave at the appointed time.

30. Thanking him in creative ways for his attempts to please you.

31. Asking for forgiveness and saying, "I was wrong and will try to change."

32. Actually changing where you should.

33. Working with him on his projects or . . .

34. Reading the literature he asks you to read and sharing your insights.

35. Letting him know when he has tough decisions to make, and even when they are not so tough, that you really believe he will choose the right thing and that you will wholeheartedly support him in whatever decision he makes, provided the decision does not violate clearly revealed biblical principles. Be his best cheerleader and fan club.

36. Buying gifts for him . . .

37. Watching football or some other sporting events with him and trying to really manifest an interest.

38. Cooking creatively and faithfully.

39. Keeping the house neat and clean.

40. Being appreciative and cooperative when he holds you, caresses you, or kisses you.

41. Lovingly giving him your input when you think he is in error.

42. Offering constructive suggestions when you think he could improve or become more productive. Don't push or preach or do this in such a way that you belittle him, but seek positive and nonthreatening ways to help him become more fully the man God wants him to be.

43. Running errands gladly.

44. Seeking to complete, not compete with him. Be the best member of his team and seek to convince him that you are just that.

45. Being lovingly honest with him—no backdoor messages or withholding of the truth that may hinder your present or future relationship.

46. Being willing to see things from his point of view by putting the best interpretation on what he does or says until you have proof that proves the contrary.

47. Pampering him and making a fuss over him.

48. Being happy and cheerful.

49. Refusing to nag.

50. Gently brushing his leg under the table.

51. Having candlelight and music at dinner.

52. Indicating you want to be alone with him to talk or just lie in each other's arms.

53. Giving an "I promise you" wink.

54. Going for a walk with him.

55. Letting him know you are lonely when he is out of town or away from you for a period of time.

56. Relating what happened to you during your day.

57. Sharing your fears, concerns, joys, failures, etc.

58. Seeking to support your ideas with biblical insights and good reasons.

59. Refusing to cop out, blow up, attack, blame shift, withdraw, or exaggerate when he seeks to make constructive suggestions or discuss problems.

60. Giving him your undivided attention when he wants to talk.

61. Discussing the meaning of certain Bible passages.

62. Cheerfully staying up until ____ o'clock to solve a problem or share his burdens.

63. Holding him close while expressing genuine concern and tangible and vocal love when he is hurt, discouraged, weary, or burdened.

64. Being eager to share a good joke or some other interesting information you have learned.

65. Working in the yard, painting a room, washing the car, etc., together.

66. Planning vacations and trips together.

67. Wanting to keep family memorabilia, newspaper clippings, church releases, etc., that have to do with your husband.

68. Bragging about him, his accomplishments, and how good a husband he is to other people.

69. Joining him in a team ministry at the church.

70. Doing a Bible study or a Bible research project together.

71. Doing a good job in bookkeeping family finances.

72. Helping prepare the income tax report.

73. Keeping in touch through letters with your family and friends.

74. Keeping yourself attractive and neat.

75. Inviting other people in for dinner and fellowship.

76. Developing and using the spiritual gifts God has given you.

77. Asking him to pray with you about something specific.

78. Managing to stay within the family budget and even save some for special surprises.

79. Being excited about sharing the gospel with others, answered prayer, or helping other people.

80. Making a list for him of things that need to be done around the house.

81. Being satisfied with your present standard of living, furniture, or equipment when he can provide no more.

82. Not making nostalgic comments about your father's way of doing things, which may seem to imply that you think your father was a much better man than your husband.

83. Acknowledging that there are some specific areas or ways in which you need to improve.

84. Taking care of his clothes so that he is always well dressed.

85. Appreciating and helping his mother, father, and relatives.

86. Refusing to disagree with him or confront him in the presence of others.

87. Cooperating with him in establishing family goals and procedures, and then fulfilling them.

88. Being silly and unconventional at times in your lovemaking.

PARENTING COMMITMENTS

Please review these biblically based parenting principles; discuss them with each other and jointly commit yourself to following these principles when you do have children. Discuss with each other what you think these principles mean and whether you are in agreement with each other about implementing these principles as you have children.

RATING SCALE:
3 = I agree completely
2 = I mostly agree
1 = I mostly disagree

Use the same rating scale to rate how you think your spouse would rate himself or herself on each of these principles.

	You	Partner
1. I will seek to make sure my expectations for our children are realistic. I will evaluate my expectations in light of the Bible. (Gen. 33:12–14; Matt. 18:10; 1 Cor. 13:11)	____	____
2. I will love my children unconditionally. (Gen. 7:7; 1 John 4:10, 19)	____	____
3. I will look for opportunities where I can commend my children. I will express appreciation for them frequently. (Phil. 1:3; 1 Thess. 1:2; 2 Thess. 1:3)	____	____
4. I will seek to avoid criticizing my children without first expressing appreciation for their good points.	____	____
5. I will give my children freedom to make decisions where serious issues are not at stake. My goal is to bring my children to maturity in Christ and not to dependence upon me. (Prov. 22:6; Eph. 4:13–15; 6:4; Col. 1:27–28)	____	____

6. I will refuse to compare my children with others. (1 Cor. 12:4–11; 2 Cor. 1:12–13; Gal. 6:4) ____ ____

7. I will not mock or make fun of my children. I will not demean or belittle them. I will not call them dumb, clumsy, or stupid. (Prov.12:18; 16:24; Matt. 7:12; Eph. 4:29–30; Col. 4:6) ____ ____

8. I will not scold my children in front of others. (Matt. 16:22–23; 18:15; 1 Cor. 16:14) ____ ____

9. I will not make threats or promises that I don't intend to keep. (Matt. 5:37; Col. 3:9; James 5:12) ____ ____

10. I will not be afraid to say "no," and when I say it, I will mean it. (Gen. 18:19; 1 Sam. 3:13; Prov. 22:15; 29:18) ____ ____

11. When my children have problems or are a problem, I will not overreact or lose control of myself. I will not yell, shout, or scream at my children. (1 Cor. 16:14; Eph. 4:26–27; 1 Tim. 5:1–2; 2 Tim. 2:24–25) ____ ____

12. I will communicate optimism and expectancy. I will not communicate by word or action that I have given up on my children or am resigned to their failure. (1 Cor. 13:7; 2 Cor. 9:1–2; Philem. v. 21) ____ ____

13. I will make sure that my children know exactly what is expected of them. ____ ____

14. I will ask my children's advice and include them in some of the family planning. (John 6:6; Rom. 1:11–12; 1 Tim. 4:12; 2 Tim. 4:11) ____ ____

15. When I make mistakes with my children, I will admit it and ask for their forgiveness. (Matt. 5:23–24; James 5:16) ____ ____

16. I will have family conferences where I will discuss family goals, projects, vacations, devotions, chores, disciplines, complaints, suggestions, and problems.

          ____   ____

17. I will welcome contributions from my children. (Ps. 128; Prov. 15:22; Titus 1:6–8; James 3:13–18)

          ____   ____

18. I will assess my children's areas of strength and then encourage them to develop these. (2 Tim. 1:16; 4:5, 1 Peter 4:10)

          ____   ____

19. I will give my children plenty of tender loving care. I will be free in my expression of love by word and deed. (John 13:34; 1 Cor. 13:1–8; 16:14; 1 Thess. 2:7–8)

          ____   ____

20. I will practice selective reinforcement. When my children do something well, I will commend them. I will especially communicate when their attitudes are what they should be. (Eph. 1:15; Col. 1:3–4; 1 Thess. 1:3–10; Philem. vv. 3–5)

          ____   ____

21. I will be more concerned about Christian attitudes and character than I will be about performance, athletic skills, clothing, external beauty, or intelligence. (1 Sam. 16:7; Prov. 4:23; Matt. 23:25–28; Gal. 5:22–23; 1 Peter 3:4–5)

          ____   ____

22. I will have a lot of fun with my children. I plan to have many fun times and many special events with my children. I will have a list of fun things my family can do. (Ps. 128; Prov. 5:15–18; 15:13; 17:22; Eccl. 3:4; Eph. 6:4; Col. 3:21)

          ____   ____

23. I will help my children learn responsibility by administering discipline fairly, consistently, lovingly, and promptly. (1 Sam. 3:13; Prov. 13:24; 19:18; 2:15)

          ____   ____

24. I will look upon each of my children as a human becoming as well as a human being. I will look upon the task of raising children as a process that takes years to complete. (Prov. 22:6; Isa. 28:9–10; 1 Cor. 15:58; Gal. 6:9; Eph. 6:4) ____ ____

25. I will live my convictions consistently. My children will learn by observing my example as well as by listening to my words. (Deut. 6:4–9; Phil. 4:9; 1 Thess. 2:10–12; 2 Tim. 1:5, 7) ____ ____

26. I recognize that I will be responsible to prepare my children for life in this world and in the world to come. (Deut. 6:4–9; Ps. 78:5–7; Eph. 6:4; 2 Tim. 3:15–17) ____ ____

27. I will be sensitive to the needs, feelings, fears, and opinions of my children. (Matt. 18:10; Col. 3:21) ____ ____

28. I will treat my children as though they are respected by me. (Matt. 18:5–6) ____ ____

29. I will avoid the use of angry or exasperated words. (Prov. 15:1; Eph. 4:31–32) ____ ____

30. I will maintain the practice of daily Bible reading, discussions, and prayer. (Deut. 6:4–9; Pss. 1:1–3; 78:5–8; 119:9, 11; Eph. 6:4; 2 Tim. 3:15) ____ ____

31. I will be thoroughly involved in a biblical church. (Eph. 4:11–16; Heb. 10:24–25) ____ ____

32. I will make my home a center of Christian hospitality where my children will be brought into frequent contact with many Christians. (2 Kings 4:8–37; Rom. 12:13; Heb. 13:1–2) ____ ____

33. I will make it easy for my children to approach me with problems, difficulties, and concerns. I will be a good listener when they need me. I will give my children my undivided attention. I will avoid being a mind reader, an interrupter, or a critic. I will show an interest in whatever interests my children. I will make myself available when my children need me—even if I am busy. (1 Cor. 9:19–23; Phil. 2:3–4; James 1:19–20; 3:16–18; 1 John 3:16–18)   ____   ____

34. I will seek to bring my children to a saving knowledge of Jesus Christ. I will become all things to my children that I might win them to and for Christ. God, of course, must do the saving, bring conviction, and give repentance and faith. I recognize that I may provide the environment in which God saves by my prayers, godly speech and example, family devotions, and involvement in a sound, biblical church. (Deut. 6:4–9; Mark 10:13–14; Rom. 10:13–17; 3:1; 1 Cor. 1:18–21; Eph. 6:4; 2 Tim. 1:5–7; 3:14–17)   ____   ____

RATE YOUR MARRIAGE

This inventory is designed to evaluate how you are doing in your marriage relationship and to identify problem areas so that you may work on correcting them. The inventory will be most beneficial if you take it individually and then sit down and discuss your respective answers to each question. Seek to understand clearly your spouse's reasons for giving the rating that he or she did. If your ratings pinpoint some difficulties, focus on how to resolve problems. Don't just attack or blame your spouse. It will be of no benefit for you to defend yourself. Remember, God does have a solution to every problem if you will only handle your problems and seek to solve them in a biblical way. View and use this inventory in a constructive way.

RATING SCALE:
4 = Always
3 = Often/frequently
2 = Sometimes
1 = Seldom
0 = Never

Write the number that describes what you judge to be true of your marriage in the blank following each question.

1. Does the fact that Jesus Christ is Lord manifest itself in practical ways in your marriage? _____

2. Do you use the Bible to determine your convictions, decisions, and practices in life in general and marriage in particular? _____

3. Do you and your spouse study the Bible and pray together? _____

4. Do you worship God together with other believers? _____

5. Do you serve God together in activities that will build up the church and honor Christ? _____

6. Do you and your spouse seek to please one another? _____

7. Do you ask for forgiveness when you have done something wrong? ____

8. Do you take full responsibility for your thoughts, actions, and reactions? ____

9. Do you allow your spouse to disagree with you without becoming nasty or punishing him or her? ____

10. Do you allow your spouse to make mistakes without becoming nasty or punishing him or her? ____

11. Do you focus on the things that are commendable, praiseworthy, and good about your spouse? ____

12. Do you express appreciation to your spouse in tangible ways? Do you express gratitude and thanks? ____

13. Do you communicate in an in-depth way with each other daily? ____

14. Do you express your opinions, ideas, plans, aspirations, fears, feelings, likes, dislikes, views, problems, joys, frustrations, and annoyances to each other? ____

15. Do you and your spouse understand each other when you try to express yourselves? ____

16. Do you do many different things together and enjoy being with each other? Are you involved in common projects? ____

17. Do you show love in many practical and tangible ways? ____

18. Do you still court one another by occasional gifts, unexpected attention, etc.? ____

19. Is your conversation pleasant and friendly? ____

20. Do you pray for one another, support, and seek to encourage one another? ____

21. Can you discuss differing viewpoints on values, priorities, religious convictions, politics, etc., without becoming irritated? ____

22. Do you anticipate sexual relations with your spouse? ____

23. Are your sexual desires compatible? ____

24. Do you freely discuss your sexual desires with your spouse? ____

25. Do you agree about the way money should be spent? ____

26. Do you think your spouse is as concerned about your views on the way money should be spent as he or she is about his or her own? ____

27. Do you agree on how to bring up children? ____

28. Do you refuse to lie to your spouse; are you building your relationship on speaking the truth? Can your spouse put full confidence in whatever you say, knowing that you really mean what you say? ____

29. Do you have a good relationship with your in-laws? Do you appreciate them? ____

30. Do you really respect your spouse? ____

31. Are you glad to introduce your spouse to friends and associates? ____

32. Do you control yourself when you are moody so that you do not disrupt your relationship and inflict your moodiness on others? ____

33. Do you seek to change your specific habits that may cause discomfort or displeasure to your spouse? ____

34. Do you make your relationship with your spouse a priority matter? ____

35. Do you treat your spouse with respect and dignity? ____

36. Do you accept corrective criticisms graciously? ____

37. Do you agree concerning the roles and responsibilities of husband and wife? ____

38. Are you willing to face, discuss, and look for scriptural solutions to problems without blowing up or attacking your spouse or dissolving into tears?   _____

39. Do you maintain your own spiritual life through Bible reading, prayer, regular church attendance, and fellowship with God's people?   _____

Total: _____

Put a circle around the number of any of the previous items that give you any concern about your relationship.

COMMUNICATION TEST 1

This test is based on the principles for good communication as given by the apostle Paul in Ephesians 4:25–32. Rate yourself and your spouse on each category. Discuss your ratings and the reasons for them with each other. Seek to improve all ratings of 3 or higher.

RATING SCALE:
5 = Regularly
4 = Frequently
3 = Sometimes
2 = Rarely
1 = Never

Hindrances to Good Communication

	You	Spouse
1. Deliberate untruth	___	___
2. Exaggeration	___	___
3. Misrepresentation	___	___
4. Promise breaking	___	___
5. Exploding, shouting	___	___
6. Silence, withdrawal, retreating, tears	___	___
7. Abusive speech	___	___
8. Gossip	___	___
9. Complaining, grumbling	___	___
10. Quarrelsome speech	___	___
11. Defensive speech, excuse making, blame shifting	___	___
12. Self-centered, boastful speech	___	___
13. Hasty, presumptuous, know-it-all speech	___	___
14. Nitpicking, fault-finding speech	___	___
15. Constant, backdoor messages	___	___

COMMUNICATION TEST 2

Rate yourself and your spouse on each category. Discuss your ratings and the reasons for them with each other. Seek to improve all ratings of 3 or lower.

RATING SCALE:
5 = Regularly
4 = Frequently
3 = Sometimes
2 = Rarely
1 = Never

Communication Prompters

	You	Spouse
1. Nonverbal communication regularly (touch, hugs, smiles, etc.)	___	___
2. Sharing time daily	___	___
3. Fun time weekly (recreation, common interests, lots of laughs)	___	___
4. Daily dealing with and resolving conflicts	___	___
5. Quick to ask for forgiveness	___	___
6. Genuine concern	___	___
7. Quick to grant forgiveness	___	___
8. Constructive speech	___	___
9. Use of first-person personal pronouns (singular) when dealing with problems and conflicts	___	___
10. Properly timed speech	___	___
11. Truthfulness (honesty, makes sure of facts)	___	___
12. Allows for differences	___	___

13. Careful listening (without interruption, undivided attention, makes sure really understands spouse) ____ ____

14. Expresses praise, appreciation, compliments, respect ____ ____

15. Gives encouragement when spouse is discouraged ____ ____

16. Expresses interest in spouse's personal projects, hobbies, etc. ____ ____

17. Communicates love in the primary love language of spouse ____ ____

(16)

One-Year Checkup

*I*n preparation for this session, complete the following assignments. Many of these assignments will take a good deal of time and will need to be started several days or weeks before your class session. Therefore, use them as part of your devotions and work on them on a regular basis. Don't wait until a few days before the session to start.

Assignments:

1. Plan a fun day on which you will do something mutually enjoyable at least once a month. Keep a record of what you do and how you enjoyed or didn't enjoy it.

2. During the month preceding this session, do the *One Plus One Equals One* study in this manual.

3. During the week before this session, you and your spouse each fill out the *Common Interests* form reflecting what is happening now in your relationship. Each of you specify whether you are satisfied or unsatisfied with the common interests you have.

4. During the week before this session, each of you take *Communication Test 1* and *2* reflecting what is happening in this area in your relationship.

5. During the week preceding this session, each of you will *Rate Your Marriage*. After taking this evaluation, circle the numbers of the items that are of any concern for you. You've taken this test on two other occasions, but it serves as a constant means of

evaluation concerning your relationship. (Suggestion: use it as a self-evaluative tool for the rest of your life.)

6. During the week before this session, complete the assignments labeled *Personal Inventory 1* and *2*.

7. Write down any issues you want to discuss. If problems arise that you are not able to resolve, call your counselor or teacher before they multiply or intensify.

ONE PLUS ONE EQUALS ONE

Write out your answers individually. Then get together with your spouse, share, and discuss them. Agree on any action you want to take as a result of your sharing.

1. When the Bible speaks of marriage as a one-flesh relationship, I think it means:

2. When I think of oneness in marriage, I think of:

3. In our marriage, I have felt distanced from you when:

4. Sometimes it is hard for us to achieve intimacy because:

5. Our oneness could be further enhanced by:

6. In our relationship I have felt very close to you when:

7. We are developing oneness in our relationship by:

8. Our oneness in marriage has been, or is being, hindered by:

9. Some of the happiest moments I have in our relationship are:

10. Three words I would use to describe our relationship are:

11. Before either of us dies, I would like to see the following desires for our marriage fulfilled:

12. On the day of our wedding, my thoughts and feelings about you were:

COMMON INTERESTS

How do you and your spouse participate in the following activities? Check the appropriate space for each item. Let this inventory challenge you if you need to be challenged in terms of common interests.

	Together	Both but not together	One exclusively	One primarily	Neither
Church (attendance and service)					
Reading					
Competitive sports (tennis, volleyball, etc.)					
Noncompetitive sports (jogging, swimming, etc.)					
Spectator sports					
Outdoor activities					
Social gatherings (family, friends, church, community, etc.)					
Clubs, organizations					
Art appreciation (listening to music, visiting museums, etc.)					
Creative and interpretive art (writing, painting, etc.)					
Hobbies (collecting, gardening, sewing, etc.)					
Business and professional activities					
School functions or organizations					
Politics					
Movies					
Devotions					
Shopping					

	Together	Both but not together	One exclusively	One primarily	Neither
Table games					
Sightseeing					
Entertaining friends					
Other _____					

COMMUNICATION TEST 1

This test is based on the principles for good communication as given by the apostle Paul in Ephesians 4:25–32. Rate yourself and your spouse on each category. Discuss your ratings and the reasons for them with each other. Seek to improve all ratings of 3 or higher.

RATING SCALE:
5 = Regularly
4 = Frequently
3 = Sometimes
2 = Rarely
1 = Never

Hindrances to Good Communication

	You	Spouse
1. Deliberate untruth	____	____
2. Exaggeration	____	____
3. Misrepresentation	____	____
4. Promise breaking	____	____
5. Exploding, shouting	____	____
6. Silence, withdrawal, retreating, tears	____	____
7. Abusive speech	____	____
8. Gossip	____	____
9. Complaining, grumbling	____	____
10. Quarrelsome speech	____	____
11. Defensive speech, excuse making, blame shifting	____	____
12. Self-centered, boastful speech	____	____
13. Hasty, presumptuous, know-it-all speech	____	____
14. Nitpicking, fault-finding speech	____	____
15. Constant, backdoor messages	____	____

COMMUNICATION TEST 2

Rate yourself and your spouse on each category. Discuss your ratings and the reasons for them with each other. Seek to improve all ratings of 3 or lower.

Rating Scale:
5 = Regularly
4 = Frequently
3 = Sometimes
2 = Rarely
1 = Never

Communication Prompters

	You	Spouse
1. Nonverbal communication regularly (touch, hugs, smiles, etc.)	____	____
2. Sharing time daily	____	____
3. Fun time weekly (recreation, common interests, lots of laughs)	____	____
4. Daily dealing with and resolving conflicts	____	____
5. Quick to ask for forgiveness	____	____
6. Genuine concern	____	____
7. Quick to grant forgiveness	____	____
8. Constructive speech	____	____
9. Use of first-person personal pronouns (singular) when dealing with problems and conflicts	____	____
10. Properly timed speech	____	____
11. Truthfulness (honesty, makes sure of facts)	____	____
12. Allows for differences	____	____

13. Careful listening (without interruption, undivided attention, makes sure really understands spouse) ___ ___

14. Expresses praise, appreciation, compliments, respect ___ ___

15. Gives encouragement when spouse is discouraged ___ ___

16. Expresses interest in spouse's personal projects, hobbies, etc. ___ ___

17. Communicates love in the primary love language of mate ___ ___

RATE YOUR MARRIAGE

This inventory is designed to evaluate how you are doing in your marriage relationship and to identify problem areas so that you may work on correcting them. The inventory will be most beneficial if you will take it individually and then sit down and discuss your respective answers to each question. Seek to understand clearly your spouse's reasons for giving the rating that he or she did. If your ratings pinpoint some difficulties, focus on how to resolve problems. Don't just attack or blame your spouse. It will be of no benefit for you to defend yourself. Remember, God does have a solution to every problem if you will only handle your problems and seek to solve them in a biblical way. View and use this inventory in a constructive way.

RATING SCALE:
4 = Always
3 = Often/frequently
2 = Sometimes
1 = Seldom
0 = Never

Write the number that describes what you judge to be true of your marriage in the blank following each question.

1. Does the fact that Jesus Christ is Lord manifest itself in practical ways in your marriage? _____

2. Do you use the Bible to determine your convictions, decisions, and practices in life in general and marriage in particular? _____

3. Do you and your spouse study the Bible and pray together? _____

4. Do you worship God together with other believers? _____

5. Do you serve God together in activities that will build up the church and honor Christ? _____

6. Do you and your spouse seek to please one another? _____

7. Do you ask for forgiveness when you have done something wrong? _____

8. Do you take full responsibility for your thoughts, actions, and reactions? _____

9. Do you allow your spouse is to disagree with you without becoming nasty or punishing him or her? _____

10. Do you allow your spouse to make mistakes without becoming nasty or punishing him or her? _____

11. Do you focus on the things that are commendable, praiseworthy, and good about your spouse? _____

12. Do you express appreciation to your spouse in tangible ways? Do you express gratitude and thanks? _____

13. Do you communicate in an in-depth way with each other daily? _____

14. Do you express your opinions, ideas, plans, aspirations, fears, feelings, likes, dislikes, views, problems, joys, frustrations, and annoyances to each other? _____

15. Do you and your spouse understand each other when you try to express yourselves? _____

16. Do you do many different things together and enjoy being with each other? Are you involved in common projects? _____

17. Do you show love in many practical and tangible ways? _____

18. Do you still court one another by occasional gifts, unexpected attention, etc.? _____

19. Is your conversation pleasant and friendly? _____

20. Do you pray for one another, support, and seek to encourage one another? _____

21. Can you discuss differing viewpoints on values, priorities, religious convictions, politics, etc., without becoming irritated? _____

22. Do you anticipate sexual relations with your spouse? _____

23. Are your sexual desires compatible? _____

24. Do you freely discuss your sexual desires with your spouse? _____

25. Do you agree about the way money should be spent? _____

26. Do you think your spouse is as concerned about your views on the way money should be spent as he or she is about his or her own? ____

27. Do you agree on how to bring up children? ____

28. Do you refuse to lie to your spouse; are you building your relationship on speaking the truth? Can your spouse put full confidence in whatever you say, knowing that you really mean what you say? ____

29. Do you have a good relationship with your in-laws? Do you appreciate them? ____

30. Do you really respect your spouse? ____

31. Are you glad to introduce your spouse to friends and associates? ____

32. Do you control yourself when you are moody so that you do not disrupt your relationship and inflict your moodiness on others? ____

33. Do you seek to change your specific habits that may cause discomfort or displeasure to your spouse? ____

34. Do you make your relationship with your spouse a priority matter? ____

35. Do you treat your spouse with respect and dignity? ____

36. Do you accept corrective criticisms graciously? ____

37. Do you agree concerning the roles and responsibilities of husband and wife? ____

38. Are you willing to face, discuss, and look for scriptural solutions to problems without blowing up or attacking your spouse or dissolving into tears? ____

39. Do you maintain your own spiritual life through Bible reading, prayer, regular church attendance, and fellowship with God's people? ____

Total: ____

Put a circle around the number of any of the previous items that give you any concern about your relationship.

PERSONAL INVENTORY 1

Rate *yourself* on each of the following traits. After each word, put the number from the rating scale that most accurately describes you.

RATING SCALE:
5 = Regularly
4 = Frequently
3 = Sometimes
2 = Rarely
1 = Never

Loving   ____
Honest   ____
Sensitive   ____
Good parent   ____
Works hard   ____
Keeps his or her word   ____
Dependable   ____
Doesn't take advantage   ____
Doesn't use people   ____
Not an opportunist   ____
Plans ahead   ____
Knows where he or she is going   ____
Fair   ____
Consistent   ____
Persevering   ____
Admits wrong   ____
Teachable   ____
Analytical   ____
Compassionate   ____
Cooperative   ____
Neat   ____
Objective   ____
Patient   ____
Considerate   ____
Persistent   ____

Punctual   _____
Disciplined   _____
Sincere   _____
Courteous   _____
Creative   _____
Decisive   _____
Efficient   _____
Flexible   _____
Forgiving   _____
Generous   _____
Frugal   _____
Appreciative   _____
Hospitable   _____
Diligent   _____
Discerning   _____
Enthusiastic   _____
Courageous   _____
Conscientious   _____

Draw a circle around any rating that causes some problems in your marital relationship.

PERSONAL INVENTORY 2

Rate *your spouse* on each of the following traits. After each word, put the number from the rating scale which most accurately describes him or her.

RATING SCALE:
5 = Regularly
4 = Frequently
3 = Sometimes
2 = Rarely
1 = Never

Loving _____
Honest _____
Sensitive _____
Good parent _____
Works hard _____
Keeps his or her word _____
Dependable _____
Doesn't take advantage _____
Doesn't use people _____
Not an opportunist _____
Plans ahead _____
Knows where he or she is going _____
Fair _____
Consistent _____
Persevering _____
Admits wrong _____
Teachable _____
Analytical _____
Compassionate _____
Cooperative _____
Neat _____
Objective _____
Patient _____
Considerate _____
Persistent _____

Punctual   _____
Disciplined   _____
Sincere   _____
Courteous   _____
Creative   _____
Decisive   _____
Efficient   _____
Flexible   _____
Forgiving   _____
Generous   _____
Frugal   _____
Appreciative   _____
Hospitable   _____
Diligent   _____
Discerning   _____
Enthusiastic   _____
Courageous   _____
Conscientious   _____

Draw a circle around any rating that causes some problems in your marital relationship.